THE BRUCE LEE COLUMN
COLLECTING BRUCE LEE IN THE 1980'S
BY MICHAEL NESBITT

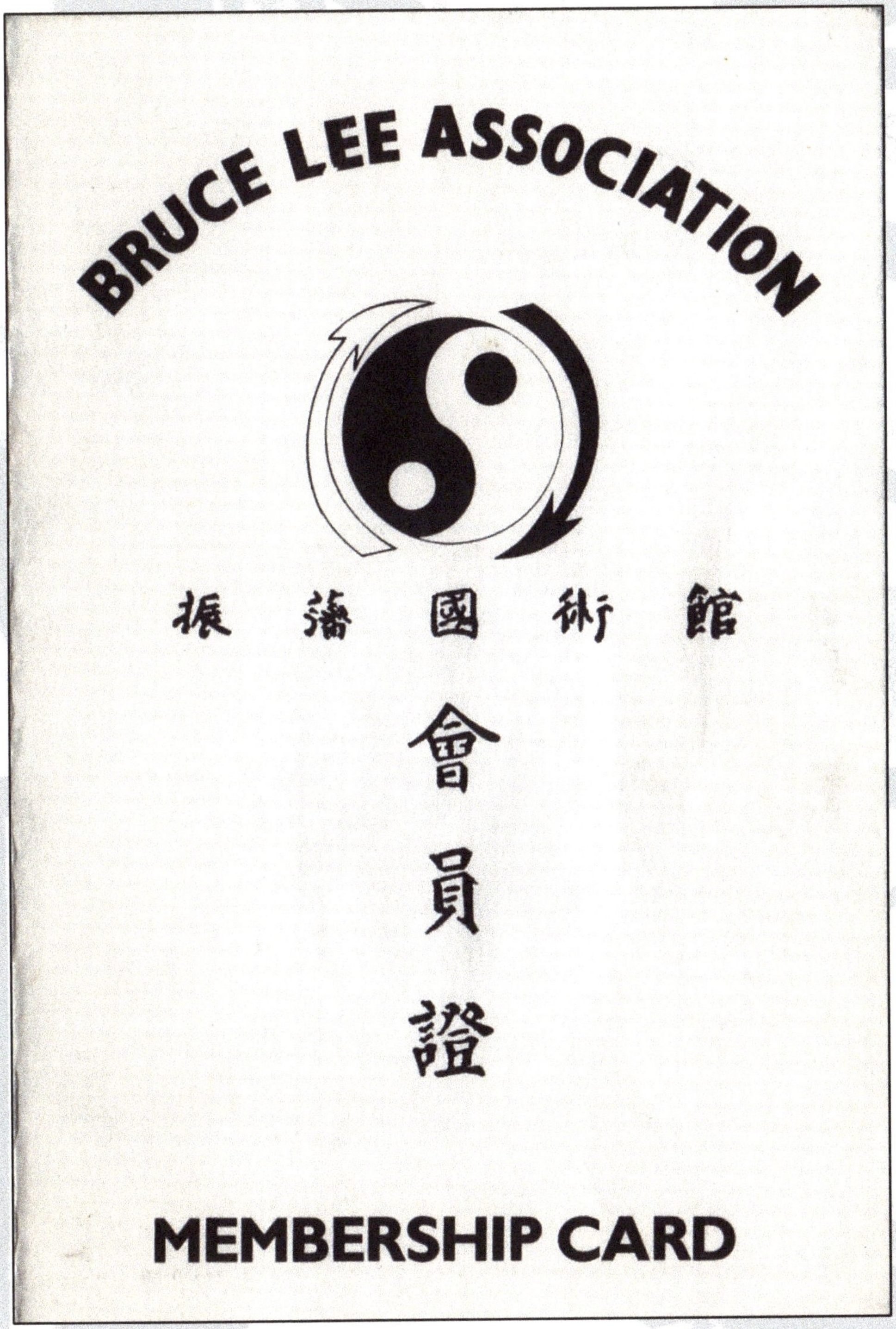

You could say I was a child of the Kung Fu Craze, with me being born in 1973, a month before Bruce Lee's untimely death. However, it wasn't until I was 13 years old, in the mid-1980s that I became a fan of Bruce Lee. And it all happened by chance. Like most kids of my generation, I was a collector of things, especially books and magazines on Ghosts, UFOs, Mysteries of the World and Doctor Who. However as a 13-year-old boy, I craved knowledge, and I found it within the pages of the Beano, Dandy, Marvel and DC comics. At the time, I didn't realise that I was about to take a journey from the fictional world of superheroes, to the factual world of superheroes, and it all started with the most unlikely of characters… Esther Rantzen.

Esther Rantzen was a relatively famous celebrity in Great Britain, and at the time she was the presenter of a consumer television program on the BBC called 'That's Life.' Every Sunday evening I would sit down in front of my granny's black-and-white TV and watch the latest episode of That's Life, and for a 13-year-old, it did a great job of keeping my focus throughout the episodes. Then one evening, as I was sitting watching the program, Esther, sitting in her regular highchair, started talking about a martial arts teacher, who was scamming people out of money for lessons. People would turn up and pay for several lessons in advance, and then the so-called martial arts teacher would start teaching them Kung Fu in hotel rooms, car parks, hallways and even on a staircase. He would ask for the money in advance for future lessons, and by the time the student knew what was happening, he wasn't prepared to give a refund. As Esther held up some martial arts magazines in which the fake Kung Fu Master advertised,

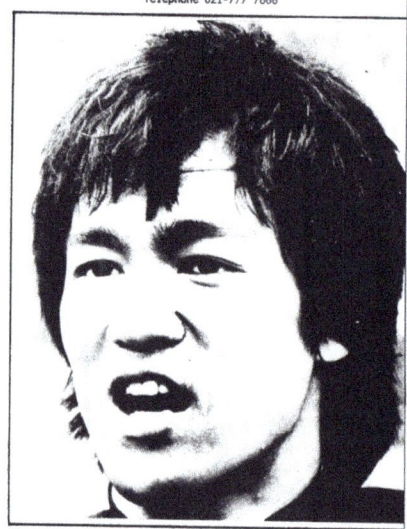

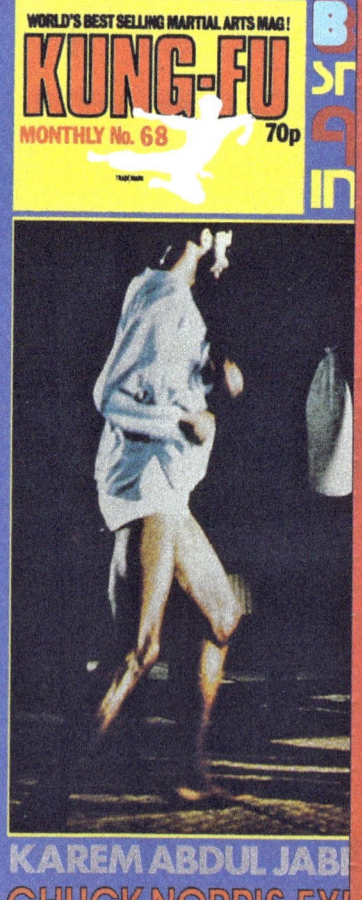

including Combat Magazine, I was transfixed. She then blurted out the now iconic words that I would remember for the rest of my life, the words that started my journey into the world of Bruce Lee, and martial arts movies. "If you're watching this," she warned; "there is someone here that wants to have a word with you!" As these words left her mouth, a young Asian man came flipping, jumping, somersaulting, and almost flying onto the screen. Throwing kicks, and punches, as the young man finished his acrobatic Kung Fu demonstration with many majestic movements, Esther went over to talk to him, and that was when I heard the name Jackie Chan for the very first time. To say I was enthralled by the whole segment was a complete understatement. The following weekend as I went food shopping with my mother, I begged pleaded and begged again, for her to buy me a martial arts magazine or two. And I don't know if it was the crying or begging that worked, but I managed to come away with an issue of Inside Kung Fu, Combat Magazine, and an American Ninja Magazine. Of course, like most young teenagers, I devoured these new magazines and read them from cover to cover, including all of the adverts. But there was one article that stood out above all the others, and that was an article about Chuck Norris and Bruce Lee. I had heard of Bruce Lee, but my young brain thought he was a fable, a fictional character made up for movies, I had no clue he was an actual real-life person. But

that was it, I was completely under the Kung Fu broom spell, even though I was some 10 years late to the party, and from that moment on I tried to get as many books and magazines on Bruce Lee as I could. Unfortunately, I had two problems, the first being that there wasn't anywhere in my area that sold books and magazines on Bruce Lee, and the second, even if there was, I just didn't have the money to get anything, so I tried every month just to get at least a copy of Combat Magazine. To this day, I still have great memories of my mother and me, going through Combat, showing her all of the adverts, and the stuff I wanted for Christmas, a Ninja Suit, a Kung Fu Suit, Ninja Stars, and Nunchaku, all being top priority. I think parents back in the 1980s were less worried about buying their children deadly weapons, well, compared to today anyway.

Living in Newcastle upon Tyne was quite difficult, as they didn't seem to be anywhere to buy anything relating to Bruce Lee or Martial Arts. That was until a couple of years later in 1987, when I found the only Martial Arts shop in the centre of Newcastle, on Low Friar Street. The shop itself was part of Doug James's Chojinkai Karate School and was situated on the top floor of a very high building, with a lot of stairs and no lift. The shop was only small; however, it did have a handful of items relating to Bruce, especially books and magazines. This is where I bought my first ever Bruce Lee Book, The Making of Enter the Dragon, written by the director of the movie Robert Clouse. It took me two days to read the book from cover to cover, and that was it, I was hooked for life. The stories within the book and the accompanying behind-the-scene photos from Enter the Dragon fired up my imagination, even more so considering I had never seen the movie up to then. I quickly followed up by reading Robert's second book, Bruce Lee the Biography, and then Linda Lee's newly released book, The Bruce Lee Story. Christmas and Birthday money, delivering papers for the local newsagents, and even the money I won playing bingo with my brother and sisters at my grannies, I would spend it all in that little Martial Arts Shop on Low Friar Street in Newcastle. Again, because it was only a small shop, it wasn't packed with Bruce Lee items, but I did manage to get copies of, Bruce Lee's Fighting Methods, The Legendary Bruce

Lee, The World of Bruce Lee volume 1 and 2, Nunchaku in Action, Skill in Two Piece Rod, Bruce Lee the Untold Story and Bruce Lee his Eternities.

Having bled the Martial Arts shop dry of all its Bruce Lee items, I managed to scrape enough money together to join the Bruce Lee Association, a fan club run by Andrew Staton, Greg Rhodes and Will Johnson. I remember the day I received my membership pack as if it were yesterday. That day in late 1988, I still consider it one of my favourite memories. Back then, the Royal Mail delivery service ran like clockwork, first-class delivery was delivered around 7 a.m. and second-class delivery was delivered at around 12 p.m. Nothing arrived first class, however, at noon, the letterbox went, and I ran upstairs to be handed a parcel by the postman. It is sad to say, but the happiness I felt at that moment was very rarely matched in adulthood, unfortunately, the older you get, the more jaded life becomes. As I sat there opening the large brown envelope, I pulled out each item one at a time, by the time I was finished, I had three issues of the Bruce Lee Association fanzines, a Bruce Lee membership card, a Bruce Lee membership badge, an amazing Bruce Lee mug, which I used for many years, and number of issues of Kung Fu Monthly. I can still remember the brand-new smell of the fanzines and KFMs. I had seen Kung Fu Monthly advertised in Combat magazine, but couldn't afford to get any, so to get three issues that day was amazing.

My insatiable hunger for collecting all things Bruce Lee took a tight grip on my life, and so I began ringing up second-hand bookshops to see if they had anything Bruce Lee or Martial Arts related. I was quite shocked really because I managed to pick up several items, including a battered copy of The Unbeatable Bruce Lee, whereupon I had to travel all the way to North Shields on the seafront to get it. Today's generation doesn't know the hardships we had to injure back in the 1980s as collectors, now it's as simple as looking on eBay to find a rare or two. Over the following year, I managed to pick up copies of other Kung Fu Monthly publications such as Bruce Lee in Action, Who Killed Bruce Lee, Bruce Lee the King of Kung Fu, and The Secret Art of Bruce Lee. I even managed to buy a full box of Bruce Lee items from someone for £20, which included nearly a full set of Kung Fu Monthlys, and a collection of Bruce Lee & JKD magazines and books from Hong Kong.

By now, I had gotten Enter the Dragon on VHS for my Birthday, and it blew my mind. I had seen nothing like it, and from

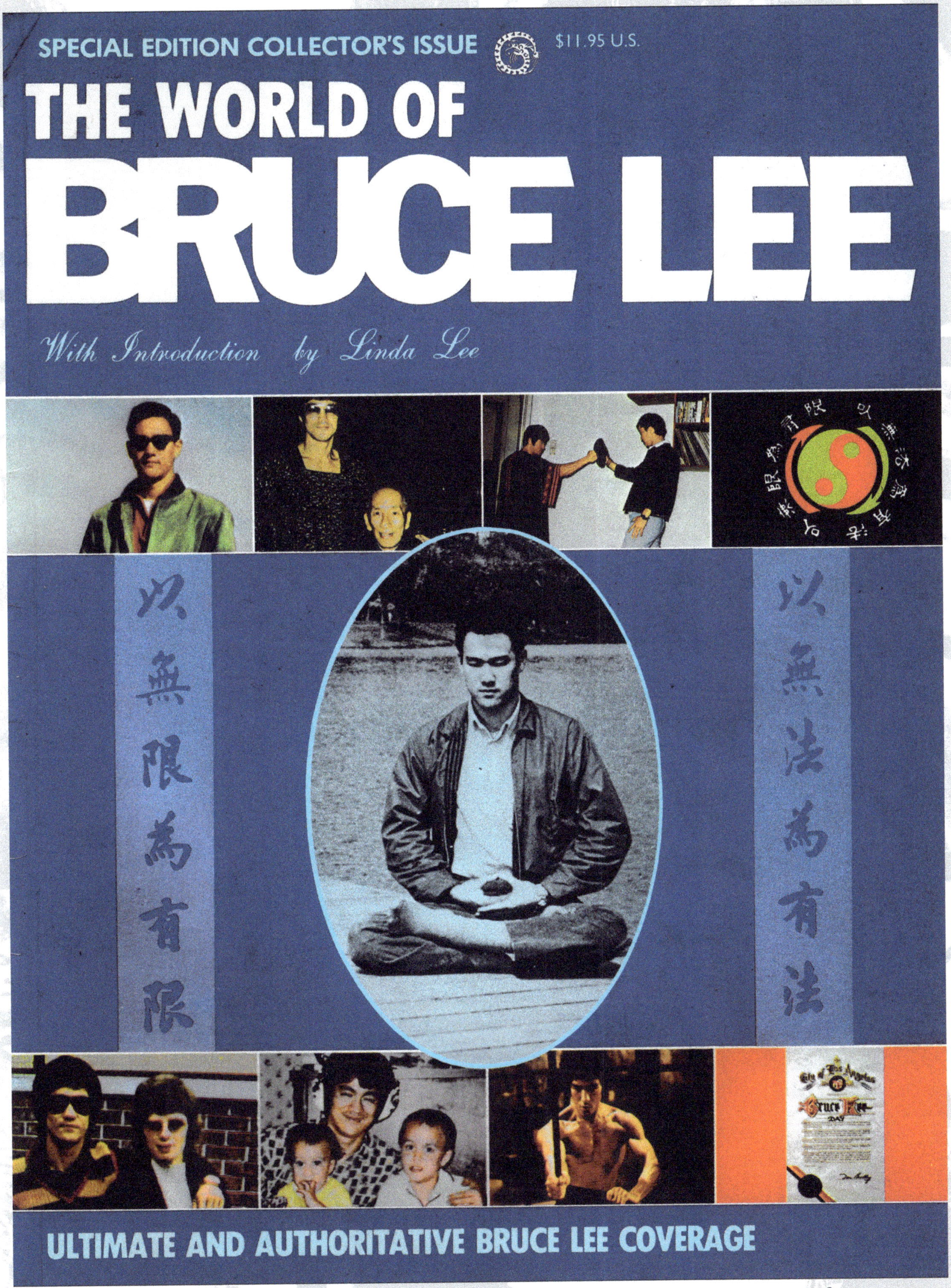
SPECIAL EDITION COLLECTOR'S ISSUE
$11.95 U.S.
THE WORLD OF
BRUCE LEE
With Introduction by Linda Lee
以無限為有限
以無法為有法
ULTIMATE AND AUTHORITATIVE BRUCE LEE COVERAGE

that moment forward I wanted to collect Bruce Lee VHS movies. Unfortunately, there simply wasn't many out there, but it still didn't stop me from scouring every Video Tape Store trying to hire out anything I could find. I eventually managed to get all the cut versions of Bruce's movie released by RANK Home Video, plus the underrated Game of Death 2, and the brilliant documentary Bruce Lee the Legend, which for me is the best documentary ever made on Bruce Lee. 1989 had arrived, and I was now 16 years old, had a job and had the money to pay for stuff, but I was struggling to find anything else relating to Bruce Lee that I could buy. And so the only course of action was to carry on calling all the local book and comic shops in the hope something would pop up. Finally, a successful phone call had the shop owner telling me that he had a book for sale called: "From Bruce Lee to the Ninjas: Martial Arts in the Movies." Bruce Lee was in the title, so within the hour I had bought the book and brought it home. It turned out to be a fascinating

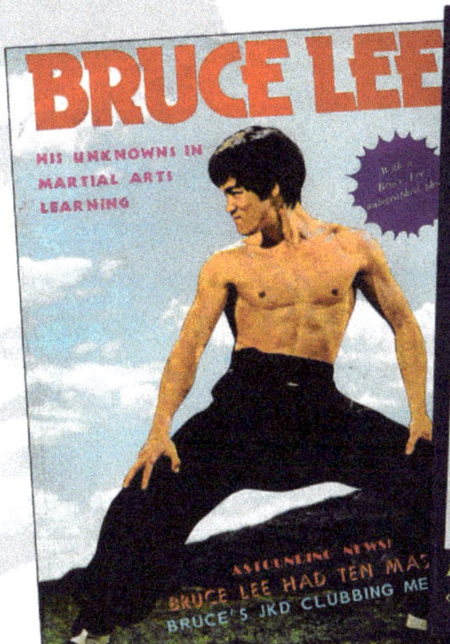
BRUCE LEE
HIS UNKNOWNS IN MARTIAL ARTS LEARNING
ASTOUNDING NEWS!
BRUCE LEE HAD TEN MA
BRUCE'S JKD CLUBBING ME
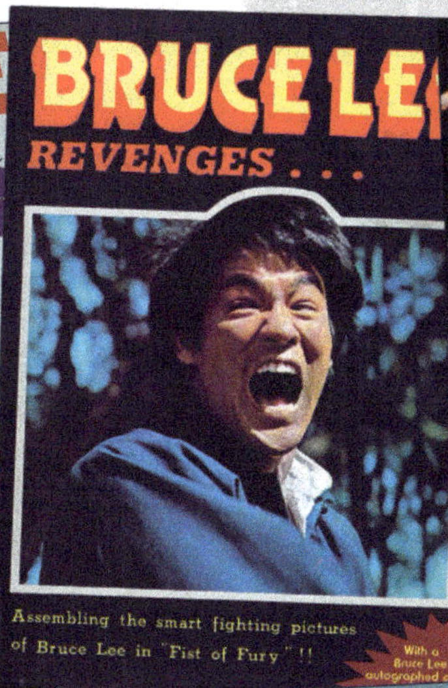
BRUCE LE
REVENGES . . .
Assembling the smart fighting pictures of Bruce Lee in "Fist of Fury"!!
With a Bruce Lee autographed pho
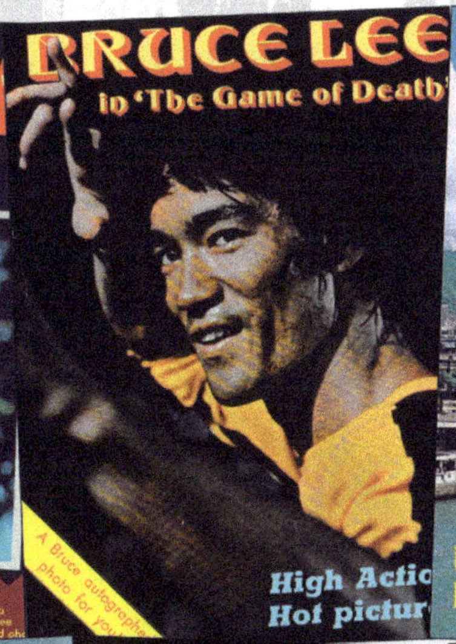
BRUCE LEE
In 'The Game of Death'
High Actio
Hot pictur
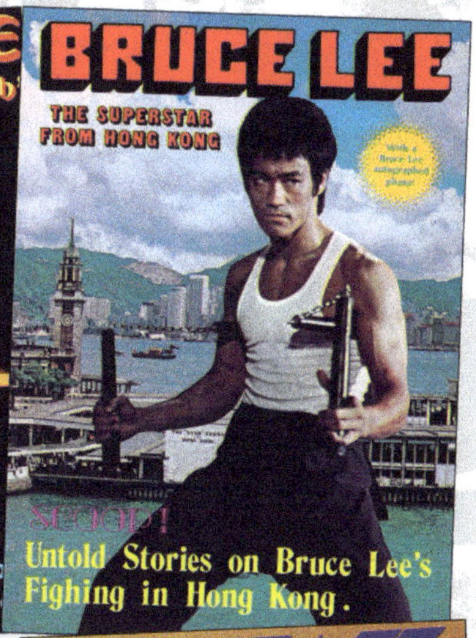
BRUCE LEE
THE SUPERSTAR FROM HONG KONG
Untold Stories on Bruce Lee's Fighing in Hong Kong.
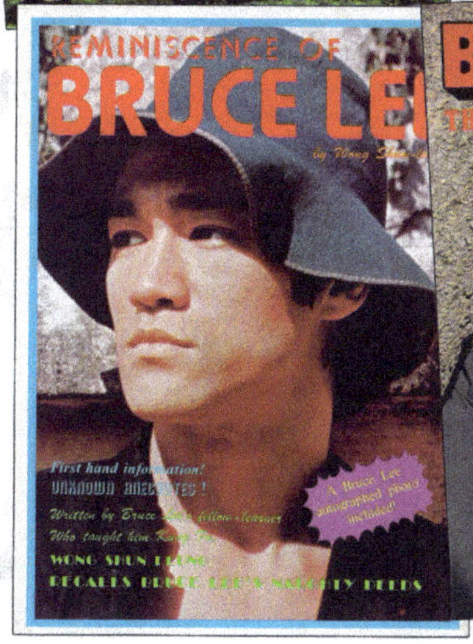
REMINISCENCE OF
BRUCE LE
A Bruce Lee autographed photo included!
WONG SHUN LEUNG
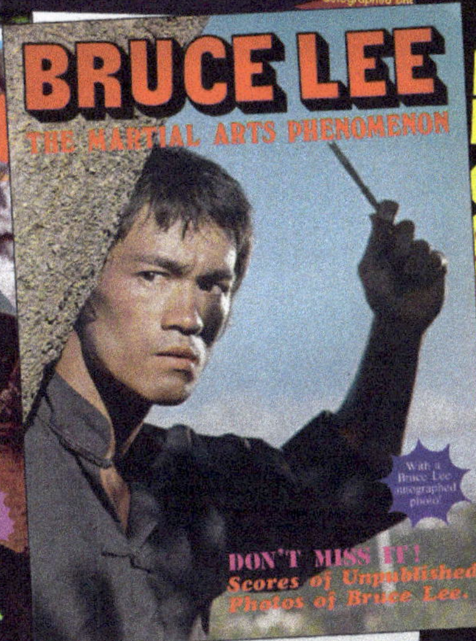
BRUCE LEE
THE MARTIAL ARTS PHENOMENON
DON'T MISS IT!
Scores of Unpublished Photos of Bruce Lee.
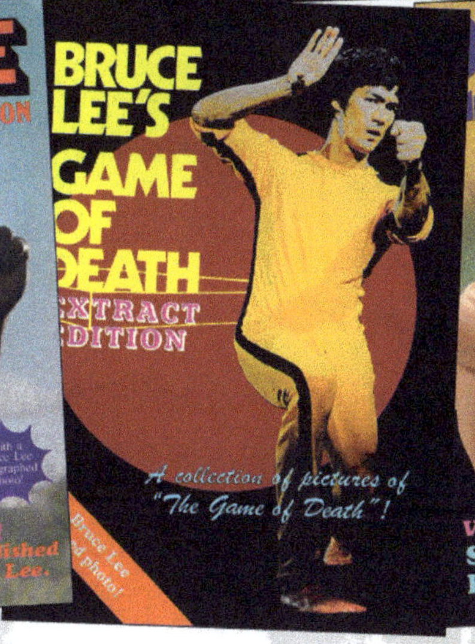
BRUCE LEE'S
GAME OF DEATH
XTRACT DITION
A collection of pictures of "The Game of Death"!
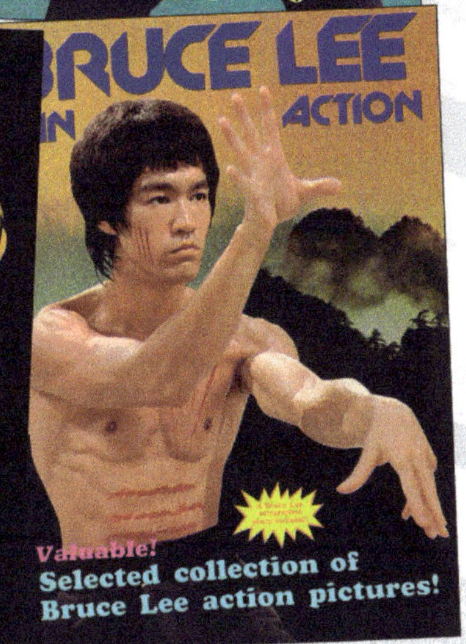
BRUCE LEE
IN ACTION
Valuable!
Selected collection of Bruce Lee action pictures!
BRUCE LEE
& JKD MAGAZINE
NO. 4
BRUCE LEE'S
SECRET TECHNIQUE
"SCISSORS KICKS"
FIGHTING BRUCE LEE POSTER INSIDE
EXCLUSIVE!
SEE HOW BRUCE LEE DIRECTS
EXPOSING THE TRIMMED SCENE OF "THE BIG BOSS"
Brand New Poster Magazine!
KUNG-FU
MONTHLY NO.1
20p
GIANT COLOUR POSTER
The Flying Fists of
BRUCE LEE
KING OF KUNG FU
THE MARTIAL ART!
BRUCE LEE SUPERSTAR
Brand New Poster Magazine!
KUNG-FU
MONTHLY NO.2
20p
GIANT BRUCE LEE POSTER INSIDE
The Spirit Of
BRUCE LEE
Lives On
Extracts from 'THE BEGINNERS GUIDE TO KUNG FU'
DAVID CARRADINE
The Grasshopper Rebel

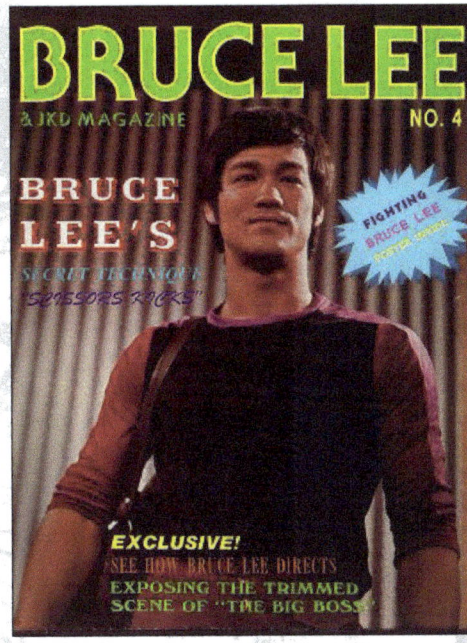

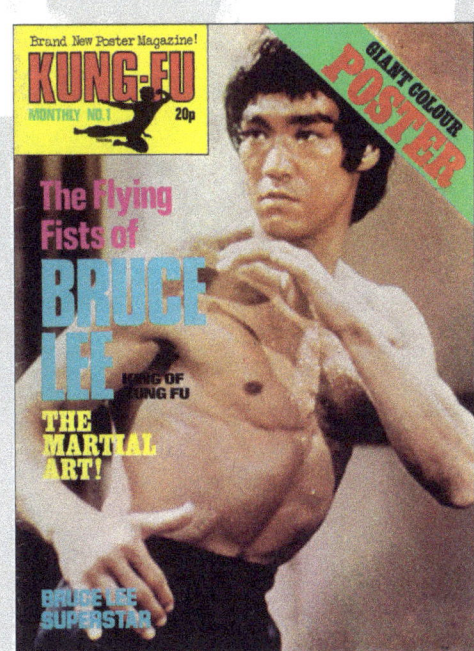

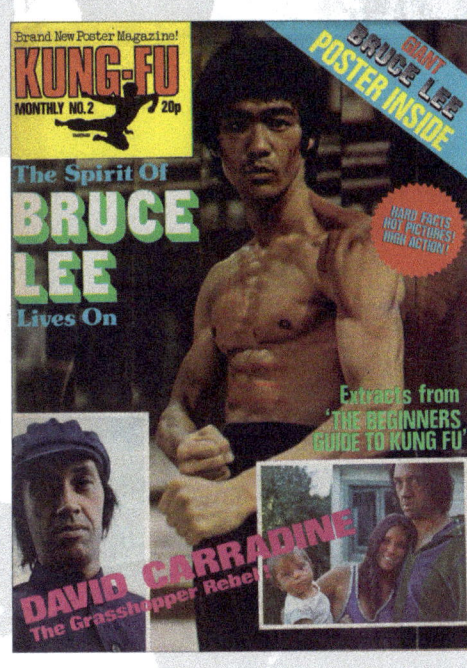

read, written by the legendary American author Ric Meyers, the book was all about Martial Arts Movie Stars and the movies they starred in. That book truly opened my eyes to Asian Action Movies, and by the end of 1989, I had joined the newly formed Jackie Chan Fan Club run by Rick Baker and Chris Alexis, and sent away for Martial Arts Black Market VHS Catalogues from the J.C.F.C. and Shaolin Video, which started me off on the next stage of my journey, collecting Asian Martial Arts Action Movies throughout the 1990s.

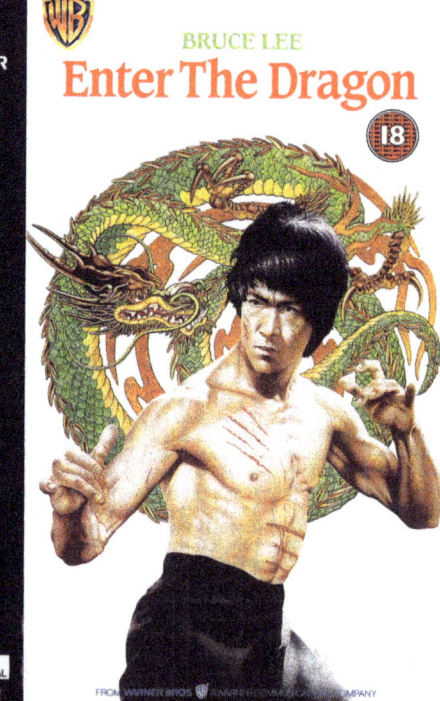

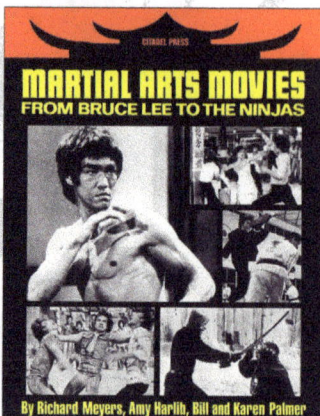

BRUCE LEE THE LEGEND

From the studio that produced the films that made him a hero to millions comes the full length documentary feature of the amazing life and death of the incomparable Bruce Lee. The film includes screen tests and out-takes never before released and demonstrates the secrets of his fighting methods with some of his most famous combat scenes.

"BRUCE LEE, THE LEGEND" traces his life right through to the final hours as seen by those who knew him best.

GOLDEN HARVEST PRESENTS A PARAGON FILM PRODUCTION "BRUCE LEE, THE LEGEND" Written By RUSSELL CAWTHORNE Narrated By JAMES B NICHOLSON Edited By JOSEPH GINGER JR.
COLOUR/1983/RUNNING TIME OF MAIN PROGRAMME 82 MINS (APPROX).

Golden Harvest Group — Distributed through Golden Communications

5014846 027621

This motion picture, including its sound track, is protected by copyright and any broadcast, public performance, diffusion, copying and editing are prohibited unless expressly authorised.
This prohibition may be enforced by legal action.

Rank Home Video, 3 Centaurs Business Park, Grant Way, Off Syon Lane, Isleworth, Middlesex, TW7 5QD, England.

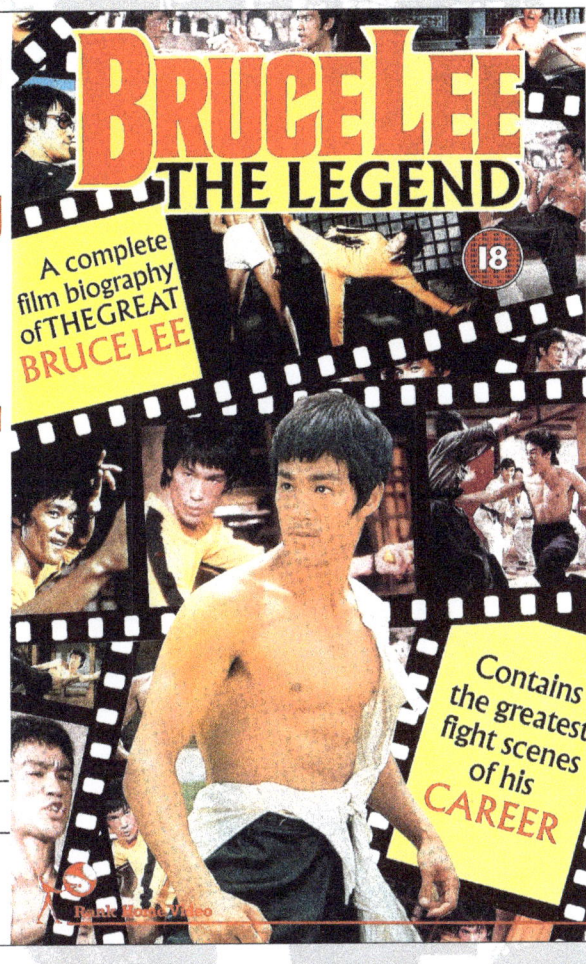

The final act. The very last legacy of the great BRUCE LEE.

GAME of DEATH II

Martial arts expert JIM KOO dies suddenly and his best friend LEE CHUN-KEUNG (Bruce Lee) is suspicious. Then Koo's coffin is "lifted" by a helicopter during the funeral. CHUEN-KEUNG hangs on to the helicopter's landing gear as it takes off but loses his grip and plunges to his death...

CHUN-KWOK, younger brother of CHUN-KEUNG, leaves the monastery to avenge his brother's death. His search leads him to the Castle of Death for the final showdown with the mastermind of an underground drug manufacturing centre...

RAYMOND CHOW PRESENTS BRUCE LEE in "GAME OF DEATH II" also starring TONG LUNG, HUONG CHENG-LI and ROY HORAN, LEE HOI-SAN. Music by CHEN HSUN-CHI. Produced by RAYMOND CHOW. Directed by NG SEE-YUAN.

PROGRAMME COPYRIGHT: © 1981 GOLDEN COMMUNICATIONS CO LTD. ALL RIGHTS RESERVED.
PACKAGE DESIGN AND SUMMARY: © 1988 RANK HOME VIDEO. ALL RIGHTS RESERVED.
COLOUR/1981/RUNNING TIME OF MAIN PROGRAMME 96 MINS.

Golden Harvest Group — Distributed through Golden Communications

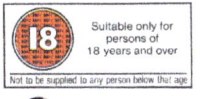 

5014846 027423

This motion picture, including its sound track, is protected by copyright and any broadcast, public performance, diffusion, copying and editing are prohibited unless expressly authorised.
This prohibition may be enforced by legal action.

Rank Home Video, P.O. Box 70, Great West Road, Brentford, Middlesex TW8 9HR England.

A GRAPHIC NOVEL
Pictures courtesy of Mike Kelly

Mike Kelly has kindly allowed us once again to show a sneak peek at his new graphic comic. We have in the past featured mikes up and coming work and his excellent illustration artwork in his "FIST OF FURY" comics. His latest work delivers again as he recreates his interpretation of Bruce Lee's classic "ENTER THE DRAGON" And I am happy that Mike has allowed me to show some exclusive pages from his forth coming issue date of release TBC at point of going to print.

© All rights reserved" the copyright holder reserves, or holds for its own use, and may not be republished without the express permission of the artist

THE WAY OF THE DRAGON
THE WRITING ON THE WALL
By Christopher Evans

I have watched "Way of the Dragon" so many times over the years and never noticed the graffiti writing on the wall. Now before I go down the rabbit hole, this may have no relation to anything other than workmen's scribble. But in this day of conspiracy's your mind will allow you to believe whatever your inner mind tells you. But when Chris asked if he could bring it to the reader's attention I said "Why not!. Some readers might be like those Reddit armchair detectives, and see some cryptic clue left by a cast member or Bruce himself. Either way, I thought this might make an interesting thought provoking article that might start debates on some of the forums.
Now over to the man that brought this to my attention.

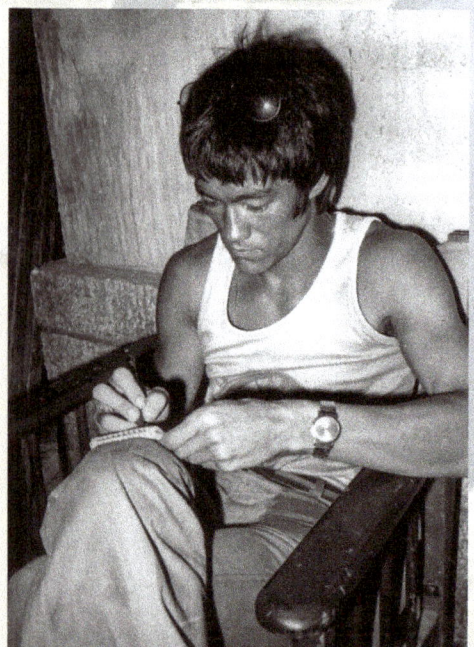

Christopher Evans gets his magnifying glass out and tries to decipher the graffiti on the Coliseum wall in the iconic fight scene in Bruce Lee's Way of the Dragon (Return of the Dragon / 猛龍過江 Měng Lóng Guò Jiāng 1972)

Yes I know what you are thinking , another Bruce Lee article to do with Way Of The Dragon Coliseum fight scene, what more is there left to be said about one of the most iconic Martial Arts battles ever committed to film?.. Well you are right, but instead of a fight scene critique I'm going to throw a puzzle out there, a particular puzzle has been frustrating me ever since I re-watched it the fight scene when I was seven years old and hopefully by sharing it with the Bruce Lee "experts" and fans out there they might become equally frustrated, or be able help solve the riddle of the chalked graffiti written on the walls.

After spending hours watching and re-watching the fight scene on DVD and Blu- Ray, pausing and pondering , I've only managed to work out one of these phrases of what the graffiti says.

The most clear and prominent phrase is : Jeet-Fan loves Linda . Jeet Jun-Fan of course being Bruce`s birth name, and Linda being his wife. So it is Bruce`s a declaration of love to Linda

Robert Lee Was Here? The OBERT can be seen on this behind the scenes photo.

A Chalk fist drawn on the wall. Used to line up the camera for continuity?

The Lee Family cat looks on

Al Bob`s Wall ? Al Bothers Wing Chun ?

The writing was meant to be seen, so it may have possibly served as a tracking continuity guide for the cinematographer/ cameraman (or

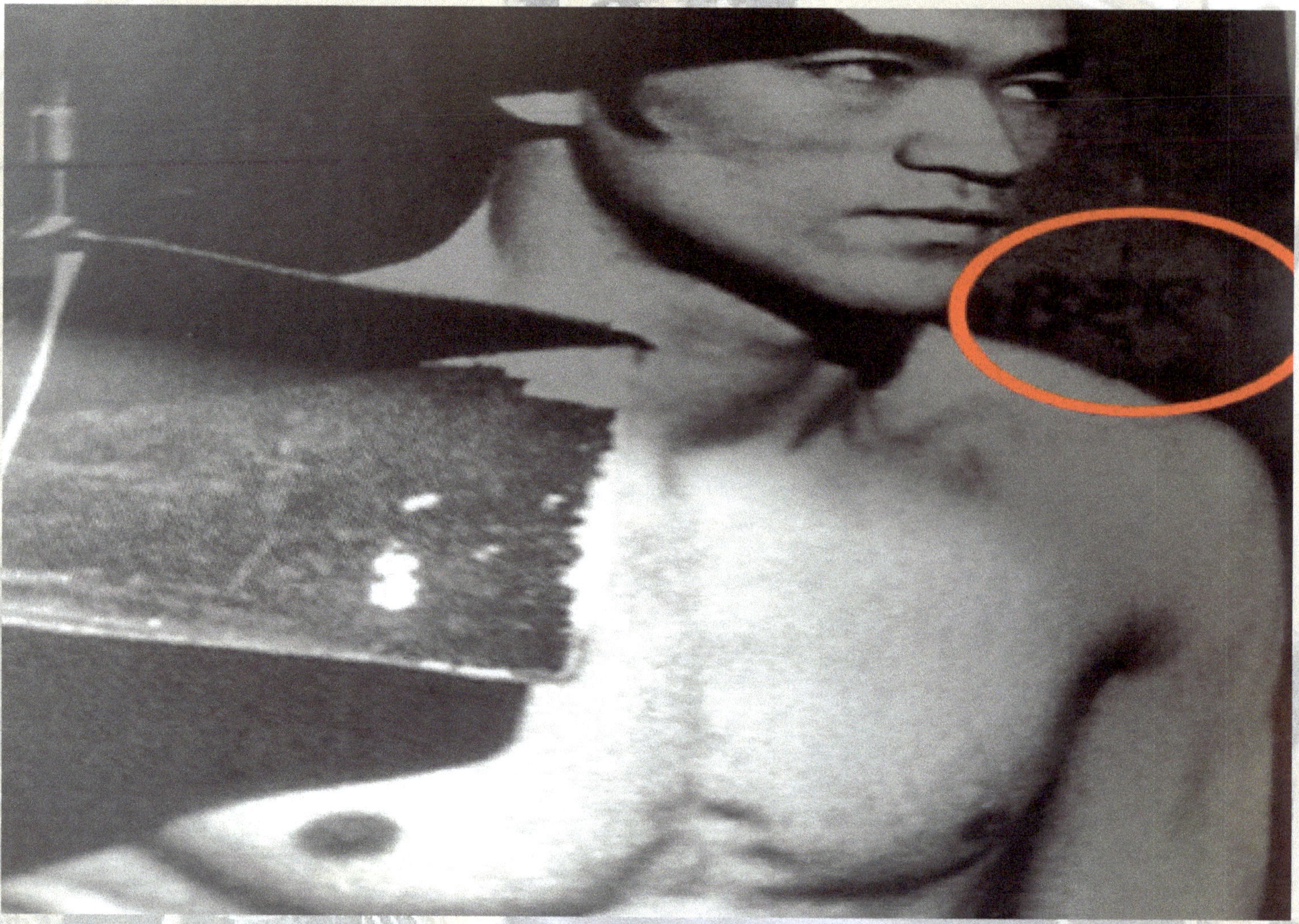

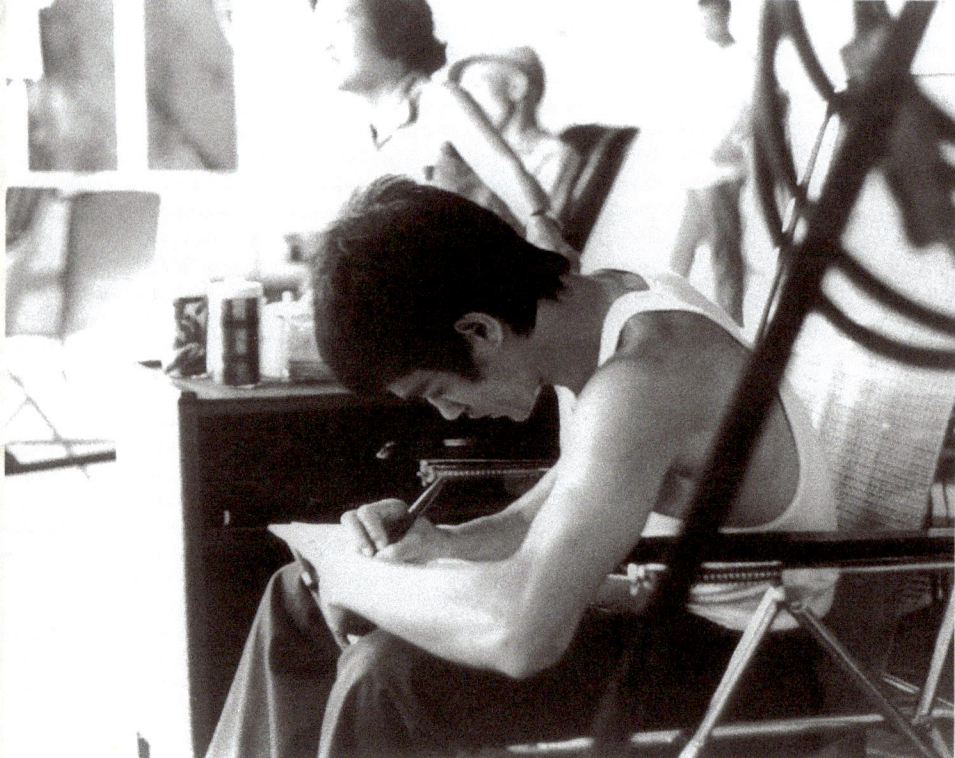

Bruce) to keep the image in frame so they could just be random phrases. So the next time you put on the Way Of The Dragon, have good hard look for the graffiti and if you have any theories, information or ideas, please feel free to contact me at brucethreeleglee@mail2world.com

THEY CALL 'EM BRUCE

By Jeff Bona

The following feature is about the many actors who have portrayed Bruce Lee in movies, TV and advertisements. In an effort to put together the most comprehensive list, I've also included those who portrayed him in ways that I can't explain. It should also be noted that the term "biopics" should be taken lightly, as ALL biopics listed are extremely sensationalized. Yes, even the ones endorsed, produced and blessed by The Bruce Lee Estate (controlled by Bruce Lee's daughter, Shannon).

Notice: This is NOT a Bruceploitation article! In other words, you won't see Dragon Lee (aka Moon Kyoung-seok) on the list – why? – well, despite capturing the essence of Bruce Lee (his image, mannerisms, Cheshire Cat-smile, clothes, etc), he never actually played Bruce Lee, unless you count The Clones of Bruce Lee, which is where I draw the line ("clones" being the key word; but Bruce Lee "ghosts" are accepted).

This article is not meant to review or rate any of the titles or performances, but that's not to say I won't go off track with some criticism here and there.

Enough chit chat. Let's not keep our Bruces waiting…

MIKE MOH

We'll start the list off with Mike Moh, the newest actor to portray Bruce Lee in a "Hollywood" movie (literally!). This Atlanta-based martial artist earned his fifth-degree Taekwondo Black Belt when he was 14, so he definitely has all the right kicks.

In 2006, Moh landed a bit part in Benny Chan's Rob-B-Hood, where he shared the screen with his idol, Jackie Chan. But it was perhaps his role as Ryu in the Street Fighter: Assassin's Fist web series (based on the popular video game) that put him on the map. Since then, he has appeared in a number of high-profile TV shows, including Marvel's Inhumans as Triton, as well as a recurring character in Fox's hit drama, Empire.

Moh portrayed Bruce Lee in Quentin Tarantino's 2019 epic, Once Upon a Time in Hollywood, opposite Brad Pitt and Leonardo DiCaprio. So what is "Bruce" doing in the film? Here's the facts: In the late 1960s, Bruce was a rising talent within an inner circle of Hollywood friends that included Sharon Tate, Jay Sebring, Roman Polanski and Steve Mcqueen. It was during this time that Bruce marketed his martial arts skills to mentor stars, choreograph films and even earned him small parts in a number of TV shows and movies (he was a marketing genius as far a I'm concerned). So having Bruce in Once Upon a Time in Hollywood makes perfect sense – after all – the film's subplot involves Charles Manson's reign of terror that left two of Bruce's friends brutally murdered. Although he looks less like Bruce than the next guy, Moh's mannerisms and speech execution are spot on, despite some oddball controversy from Bruce Lee fanatics (i.e. "The movie is BS, there's no way anyone would ever lay a hand on Bruce!"). Even Donnie Yen admitted he didn't complete watching Once Upon a Time in Hollywood when he felt "As filmmakers, I feel we should be more respectful to someone like Lee". The movie's theatrical release was cancelled in China after Shannon Lee "filed a complaint to China's National Film Administration" due to the portrayal of her late father as "arrogant" and "boastful" (via Rolling Stone).

It's worth mentioning that Moh had once auditioned for the role of Bruce Lee in 2016's Birth of the Dragon, but he lost to our next guy…

PHILIP NG WAN-LUNG

Born in Hong Kong, with a good portion of his youth spent in America, Philip Ng Wan-lung is an avid practitioner/teacher of various forms of martial arts, including Hung Gar, Wing Chun and Taekwondo. He also founded the Wing Chung Association during his attendance at the University of Illinois. As both an actor and fight choreographer, he's had a solid film career in his homeland since the early 2000s. If you look at his filmography, you'll see that he's already worked with some of the best in the industry, such as Ringo Lam, Donnie Yen, Corey Yuen, Sammo Hung and Jackie Chan.

Birth of the Dragon was a huge turning point in Ng's career. Not only was it his first Hollywood gig he's appearing/starring in, but he's also portraying Bruce Lee, so expectations for his performance were set high (playing Bruce is comparable to playing James Bond for the first time). Unfortunately, many fans dismissed Birth of the Dragon as and said it was a disgrace to Bruce's legacy – and their negative reaction towards it had nothing to do with Ng's performance. When the film made early screenings, fans were upset that the character of Bruce (Ng), the Asian, took a backseat, while the character of Steve (Billy Magnussen), the white guy, was front and center; in other words, they accused the filmmakers of racially "white washing" the film. Due to the backlash, director George Nolfi (The Adjustment Bureau) was forced to recut Birth of the Dragon, so it focused more on Bruce, and less on Steve. The irony about this alleged "white washing" thing is that Birth of the Dragon (despite its title, it's NOT a biopic) is centered around Bruce's legendary fight with Wong Jack Man (Yu Xia). This real-life, controversial bout was initiated due to Lee's teaching of Chinese martial arts to non-Chinese, which was a big no-no to Chinese traditionalists at the time. The deal behind the fight was simple: if Bruce won, he'd earn the right to teach non-Asians; if he lost, he'd have to give up these teachings. To put it simply, it's a movie about the right to educate ALL races in complete harmony.

Not surprisingly, the Bruce Lee Estate also called it inaccurate travesty, but their words are questionable because of their own 1993 biopic starring…

JASON SCOTT LEE

To mainstream audiences, Chinese/Hawaiian actor Jason Scott Lee (no relation) is the most widely recognized person to ever portray Bruce. In 1993, he starred in Rob Cohen's Dragon: The Bruce Lee Story, which was the first Hollywood project to explore Bruce's life – an the first "officially authorized" film about Bruce.

Dragon: The Bruce Lee Story is based on the 1975 book, Bruce Lee: The Man Only I Knew, by Bruce's widow, Linda Lee, who gave the film her complete blessing (at the time, she was head of The Bruce Lee Estate). If the book's title is an indication of truth, then Bruce's blood parents, blood brothers and blood sisters have no idea who the hell Bruce ever was, despite living with him during his most crucial years in Hong Kong. In fact, it's open for debate if the demonic samurai appearing in Bruce's nightmares really happened, but only Linda would know that – after all – she's the only one who knew Bruce.
Anyway, back to Jason…

To prepare for the role, Jason trained in Jeet Kune Do under the late, white Jerry Poteet, who was one of Bruce's actual students. Poteet would go on to become Jason's personal fight choreographer again for both 1998's Solider and 2003's Timecop 2: The Berlin Decision. Dragon: The Bruce Lee story was, for the most part, was adored by the general public. Some of those well-read on Bruce were quick to point out inaccuracies (and fantasy-additives, such as the demon samurai) and dismissed the acrobatic-laced choreography as bring more "Jackie Chan" than they were Bruce.
Since then, Jason has become a certified Jeet Kune Do instructor himself. Til this very day, he still uses his JKD skills, but now, they're laced with computer enhancements, as recently noted in 2016's Crouching Tiger, Hidden Dragon: Sword of Destiny. Hey, just like Bruce says,"There are no limits!"
Our next actor to portray Bruce is a Killer actor…

DANNY LEE SAU YIN

Hong Kong director/producer/star Danny Lee Sau Yin (again, no relation) is perhaps best known for starring in John Woo's 1989 ultra-violent masterpiece, The Killer, opposite Chow Yun-fat. But if you dig deeper into his decades-long career, you'll eventually come across a sleazy, Shaw Brothers-produced oddity that goes by a number of sexy titles like: 1) Bruce Lee: His Last Days, His Last Nights, 2) I Love You, Bruce Lee, 3) Bruce Lee & I and my personal favorite, 4) Sex Life of Bruce Lee.

This biopic centers on Bruce's final days, as told through the eyes of Betty Ting Pei, who reenacts her slutty ways. Here's a little background info on her so you have a clear understanding: In the late 60s/early 70s, Betty was a Taiwanese actress who was known for appearing in sleazy films, often as a sex symbol, seductress, or some sort of bad girl. Her popularity grew when she became romantically linked with Bruce towards the tail end of his film career. She became notorious to the public and Hong Kong press for being the last person to talk to – and see – Bruce just hours before his death, as he was found unconscious in her apartment, in her bedroom and on her bed. Somehow I doubt they were having a conversation about puppy dogs and ice cream. But let's get back on topic…

In the film, Danny's portrayal of Bruce involves smoking lots of weed, getting drunk, picking fights with white people, swallowing mysterious prescription drugs and having sex, lots of it, but not with Linda (if Matthew Polly's Bruce Lee: A Life is any indication, then Bruce's sexual affairs with other woman is accurate).

The Bruce Lee Estate wants you to stay away from Bruce Lee: His Last Days, His Last Nights the same way the Elvis Presley Estate wants you to stay away from Elvis' 1977 concert footage. Our next actor has been the Estate's official go-to "Bruce" for the last 12 years…

DANNY CHAN KWOK-KWAN

Stephen Chow's 2001 Blockbuster hit, Shaolin Soccer, featured a Bruce Lee-wannabe played by newcomer Danny Chan Kwok-kwan. His breakout performance in the film earned him steady work in a number of movies, most notably 2004's Kung Fu Hustle, which became another box office smash for Chow, in turn, giving Danny yet another career boost. But regardless of the characters Danny played, he was stuck as the "Bruce Lee dude in Shaolin Soccer." Film producers took note of this and Danny became the go-to guy when a "Bruce Lee" was needed for a project.

His first real portrayal as Bruce Lee came in the form of 2008's The Legend of Bruce Lee, a 50-episode series that centered on Bruce's life starting from his early Hong Kong years to his untimely death. The series, which was executively produced by Shannon Lee, is filled with so much embellished and historical inaccuracies that it makes Dragon: The Bruce Lee story look like Das Boot. But hey, gotta keep the legend alive, right? Danny's next gig as Bruce came in the form of a 90-second television commercial for Johnnie Walker Blue Label whiskey. For the advertisement, Danny's face was digitally altered to resemble Bruce as accurately as possible (the final product resembles a PS3-era video game with no evidence of Danny being present). Danny's assistance was once again needed for 2015's Ip Man 3, starring Donnie Yen. Originally, the plan was for Ip Man 3 to feature a computer generated version of Bruce (over a real guy, laced with CGI, just like they did for his favorite beverage), but due to a last minute legal threat from The Bruce Lee Estate, the CGI idea was ditched. Note: The Bruce Lee Estate owns Bruce's likeness, image, name, persona, voice, signature, DNA and the air he used to breathe. Eventually, an agreement was made between Ip Man 3 producers and The Bruce Lee Estate to bring Danny back as Bruce. Perhaps it was Danny's association with Shannon's The Legend of Bruce Lee that saved Ip Man 3 from scrapping Bruce from the storyline completely? Make sense.
Danny reprised his role as Bruce Lee in 2019's Ip Man 4.

AARIF RAHMAN

In 2010, a rising heartthrob named Aarif Rahman (aka Aarif Lee, no relation) – who is of mixed Arab, Malay and Chinese descent – portrayed Bruce in Raymond Yip and Manfred Wong's Bruce Lee, My Brother (aka The Young Bruce Lee), a Bruce Lee biopic that takes place between 1940 and 1959.

Bruce Lee, My Brother is noted for being produced by Robert Lee, Bruce's younger brother (the film even opens with an introduction by him and his older sister, Phoebe Lee), which gives the movie a sense of credibility, hence the film's title. Even before Bruce Lee, My Brother went into production, Robert approached Shannon about the details of the film's investors: "Then she didn't want to work with me. She wanted the whole deal to herself," he said. "We don't talk as much as I would like to. They don't want to collaborate with us. We are one family. There is no reason why we shouldn't collaborate. We share different parts of Bruce's life." (via South China Morning Post) Unfortunately, the film has yet to see an official release in the U.S., due to legal clashes with The Bruce Lee Estate.

Aarif never portrayed Bruce or played Bruce Lee-like characters again, but his singing and acting career continues to flourish in a number of high profile projects. He recently co-starred with Jackie Chan in 2017's Kung Fu Yoga, where he was able to show more of his fighting skills.

HO CHUNG-TAO

Ho Chung-tao, a Taiwanese actor/martial artist who goes by the screen name, Bruce Li, has played Bruce so many times, that it's nearly impossible to give you an accurate list of his Bruce-related titles. Although he's not not the first person to play Bruce (technically, some dude's sweaty back in 1972's Fist of Unicorn gets that honor), he was the first to portray him in the first ever biopic, Bruce Lee: A Dragon Story, which was a cheaply produced, 1974 Chinese production filmed months after Bruce's death. Ho would go on to play Bruce again in a handful of biopics such as 1975's Super Dragon, 1976's Story of the Dragon and 1978's The Dragon Lives.

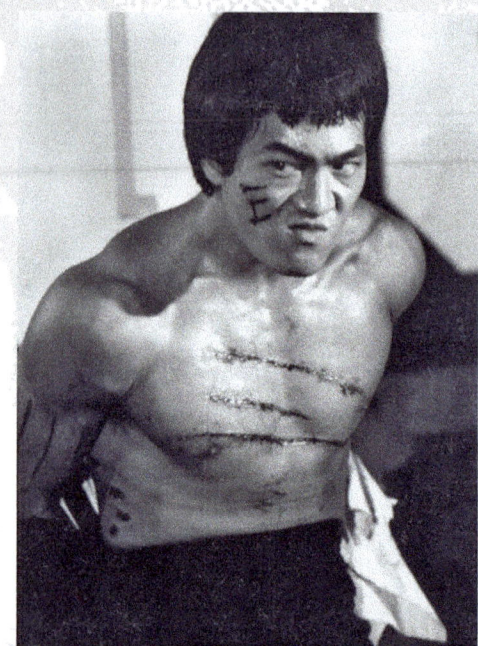

Of all Ho's biopics, the one that's considered the most legitimate was 1976's Bruce Lee: The Man, The Myth. It had a big budget, was shot on location in Hong Kong, USA, Korea and Rome, and it had one hell of a director, Ng See Yuen (The Secret Rivals), whose Seasonal Films Corporation would skyrocket both Yuen Woo-ping and Jackie Chan – with 1978's Snake in the Eagles Shadow and Drunken Master – into a new level stardom. It was because of Ho's biopic output that a planned 1975 Hollywood movie titled Bruce Lee: His Life and Legend never saw the light of day. The film was to be directed by Robert Clouse (Enter the Dragon), in association with Linda Lee. Producers had even found their "Bruce" with Alex Kwok (aka Alex Kwon). Ultimately, the project was shelved due to the oversaturated market of Chinese-made biopics. So because of Ho, Alex Kwok isn't on this list.

Ho would go on to star in a number of acclaimed projects that had little or nothing to do with Bruce. Films like 1977's Last Strike, 1979's The Golden Connection and 1981's The Chinese Stuntman, which he also directed, proved that Ho could stand on his own, without the help of his marketable idol. By mid-late 80s, Ho semi-retired from film industry, before completely quitting the scene by 1990.

HUANG CHIEN LUNG

If Ho Chung-tao is the "Walmart" of Bruce Lee-inspired actors, then Huang Chien Lung was the "Walmart Bargain Bin" of Bruce Lee-inspired actors. Ho had some oddballs in his filmography, but Huang takes the cake for making movies that resembled the cheapest Filipino exploitation films – in fact, a handful of them were actually made in the Philippines. Better known as Bruce Le, this Chinese-Burmese native – and avid martial artist – got his start as taking minor roles in a number of films produced by the famous Shaw Brothers studios.

When Bruceploitation-era was taking shape in the 70s, Huang's likeness to Bruce Lee caught the eye of producers, and he was eventually cast as Cheng Chao-an's brother in 1976's The Big Boss Part II (Bruce Lee played Cheng Chao-an in the 1971 original). The same year came Bruce's Deadly Fingers, starring Huang as a very Bruce-like character, where he teamed up with frequent Bruce Lee co-star, Nora Miao (Way of the Dragon). From this point forward, Huang would churn out titles like 1978's Enter the Game of Death (it was Fist of Fury meets Game of Death), 1980's Clones of Bruce Lee (with Dragon Lee, Bruce Lai and Bruce Thai), 1982's Bruce Strikes Back(with Hwang Jang Lee, Casanova Wong, Harold Sakata) and 1986's Future Hunters (starring Terminator 2's Robert Patrick and directed by Filipino film legend Cirio H. Santiago).But the reason why Huang is even on this list is because he actually plays Bruce Lee in 1980s Bruce – The King of Kung Fu, a highly fabricated biopic he also directed. The film features main Enter the Dragonvillain, Sek Kin, as well as Bolo Yeung (which is really nothing special, since he's in everything). Today, Huang is still going at it, but mainly behind the camera as a director. One of his recent projects include 2014's Eyes of Dawn (a redux of his 1992 film, Comfort Women) and he has just wrapped up the war movie, Bloody Hero. He's also keen on going back to martial arts movies with a dream project that would be a worthy successor to Enter the Dragon.

KIM TAI-CHUNG

If there's one guy that qualifies as a certified "Bruce Lee" actor, it's Korean martial arts star, Kim Tai-chung, who also goes by his Chinese screen name, Tong Lung.

A few years after the death of Bruce Lee in 1973, Golden Harvest Studios (the company behind all of Bruce's films) started pre-production on Bruce's incomplete film, Game of Death. Bruce had already shot the film's action finale, which meant that all that was left to shoot was… well… the rest of the damn movie. This meant they needed someone who could not only fight like Bruce, but also walk, move, and capture his overall essence.

After an exhaustive search, producers finally found their leading man in Kim Tai-chung. With the help of some cardboard cut outs, sunglasses, a prosthetic beard, Bruce's actual corpse, two or three other body doubles and footage from Bruce's other completed films, they were able to finally complete 1978's Game of Death, which was directed by Robert Clouse (Enter the Dragon). The film features a cast consisting of so many white people that's probably the most white washed movie ever made. They even threw in clips of Chuck Norris to give it a little financial boost.

Despite its sloppy finished product, Game of Death was a box office smash. The demand for more Bruce Lee was obviously evident, so Golden Harvest called Kim called back for 1981's Tower of Death (aka Game of Death II). This time around, Kim was able to fully sell himself, as he was playing his own character (let's just say he's supposed to be Bruce's brother). Together with director Corey Yuen (Raging Thunder), choreographer Yuen Woo Ping (Dance of the Drunken Mantis) and the perfect villain in Hwang Jang Lee, Tower of Death is considered one of the greatest Brucepoitation movies ever made. There was even a Korean cut of the film, which proved that Kim was becoming a star in his homeland.

After Tower of Death, Kim returned to Korea where he immediately began work on 1981's Miss, Please Be Patient (our very own yellow washed Paul Bramhall premiered the film at the Korean Culture Office in Sydney) and then came 1982's Jackie vs. Bruce to the Rescue, where Kim, as a Bruce-like character starred alongside a Jackie Chan-like character, played by Lee Siu-Ming. Even though I just went through a bunch of paragraphs regarding Kim's Bruceploiation output, the main reason he makes this list is because of his role as Bruce Lee's ghost in 1985's No Retreat, No Surrender. The film, which reunites Kim with Corey Yuen, follows the Karate Kid mold, only instead of Pat Morita, we get the ghost of Bruce Lee and better fight choreography. Above of all, No Retreat, No Surrender is predominantly remembered for launching the career of Jean-Claude Van Damme (who is now doing shit like Kill 'em All). Shortly after the release of No Retreat, No Surrender, Kim retired from acting to pursue a successful career in business. Sadly, Kim passed away in 2011, due to a stomach hemorrhage.

LEUNG SIU-LUNG

Just as producers did with Ho Chung-tao (Bruce Li) and Huang Chien Lung (Bruce Le), Leung Siu-lung was given the name Bruce Leung to help market his movies as Bruce Lee products. But unlike Li and Le, only a couple of Bruce-centric titles made their way into Leung's 65+ filmography. Legend has it that Leung once took on 13 armed attackers and defeated them single-handedly (too bad Smartphones and YouTube didn't exist back then), which eventually led to his film career. Trained in the Cantonese Opera, as well as various forms of karate and kung fu, Leung spent the most of the early 70s taking minor roles or action directing in a number of movies. It wasn't until Ng See Yuen's 1975 film, Little Superman, that Leung finally gained momentum as a kung fu star.

In 1978, Leung co-starred in Magnificent Bodyguards with Jackie Chan (who was only months away from becoming an overnight sensation). Directed by Lo Wei (The Big Boss), the film is groundbreaking for being Hong Kong's first ever 3D film (it's also infamously known for ripping off John Williams' Star Wars score). Then in 1979, Leung teamed up with Ho Chung-tao (Bruce Li) in Bruce and the Iron Finger. Although neither of the two technically connected to Bruce Lee, the "Bruce" the title is referring to is for Ho, since he's the first-billed star (makes sense to me).

But let's jump back to 1976's Dragon Lives Again, which is one of the reasons Leung is qualified for this list. Taking place after Bruce Lee's passing in 1973, this over-the-top flick starts with "Bruce Lee" (Leung) rising from his death and waking up in a mysterious after-life universe where people like James Bond, The Godfather, The Blind Swordsman, The One Armed Swordsman, Clint Eastwood, Dracula, Emmanuelle (yes, you guessed right), Zombies, Mummies and Popeye (played by Eric Tsang) roam the streets. Bruce takes on most of these guys (sometimes, in his Kato outfit).

Leung played Bruce again in the 2010 TV series, Jeet Kune Do. This time around, he portrays an elderly version of Bruce who mentors a character played by Chen Tian Xing (Nunchucks), who actually happens to be one of the newest additions of Bruceploitation era.

For the most part, Leung has had a steady career that still goes strong, but it was his memorable role as "The Beast" in Stephen Chow's Kung Fu Hustle that gave him a second wind of success not seen since his 70s glory days.

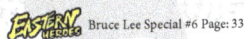

STEPHEN AU KAM-TONG

In 1999, rising Hong Kong actor Stephen Au Kam-Tong directed, starred-in and wrote What You Gonna Do, Sai Fung?, which focused on Bruce Lee's turbulent years in Hong Kong during the late 1950s. If you're wondering who the film's title is referring to, here's the explanation: In the film, Stephen's character doesn't go by the name Bruce, he goes by the name Sau Fung (or Sai Fon), which was Bruce's childhood name that meant Little Unicorn.

It was said that Bruce's family gave him this nick name (a substitute for his real name, Lee Jun-fan) which was actually a girl's name. They believed that evil spirits did not like boys in the family (their firstborn was a son who died in infancy). So, by calling him Sau Fung, they were able to trick demonic spells into thinking Bruce was female.

I've never seen What You Gonna Do, Sai Fung?, but judging from the footage, Stephen is almost a spitting image of a late 1950s-era Bruce Lee. Since Stephen holds a Black Belt in Karate, he's probably not too shabby in the action department either.

Prior to What You Gonna Do, Sai Fung?, Stephen appeared in yet another 1992 Bruce Lee biopic (not as Bruce), which is the subject of our next Bruce Lee actor. Today, Stephen is still very active in the industry. Some of his film's include 2000's The Blood Rules, 2009's Overheard, 2014's That Demon Within and just recently, 2016's Three.

DAVID WU DAI-WAI

I'm going to struggle with this one. All I have to say is thank God for Wikipedia… David Wu Dai-Wai (aka Wu-Man) is Chinese-American actor and TV personality. In 1992, he took a stab at playing Bruce Lee in the ATV series, Spirit of the Dragon.

I've never seen the series, but there is a character named Linda, played by Gwennie Tam (reverse white washing?). Of special note, the series features Lau Kar-leung, Nick Cheung, Eddy Ko Hung and of course the guy you just read about, Stephen Au.

Since 1985, David has had a solid career as he's appeared in a number of films, including 1990's Tiger Gage 2, 1991's Robotrix, 1995's Full Throttle and 1996's Temptress Moon.

JIANG DAI-YAN

There have been many of child actors – some infants, possibly some fetuses – who have played Bruce, but I'm excluding them because their roles weren't substantial enough (even if they were included, we wouldn't be able to properly identity them).

When the original Ip Man movie came out in 2008, its trailers, posters, TV spots and other advertising material

were branded with the words "Mentor of Iconic Legend Bruce Lee" – it was as if both Ip Man, the master of Wing Chun, and Donnie Yen, a top martial arts action star, were living in the shadow of Bruce Lee (even Donnie himself has had his share of Bruce-like performances in the 1995 Fist of Fury TV series, as well as 2010's Legend of the Fist). If anything, it was proof that the words "Bruce Lee" were a powerful marketing tool.

Ip Man would go on to become a box office smash and its leading man, Donnie Yen, went from star to international superstar (for more on this, read How 'Ip Man' made Donnie Yen 'The Man'). Instantly, the public wanted more Ip Man. They also wondered if a Bruce Lee character would be making an appearance in future Ip Man sequels. Let's face it, most of the general public wouldn't even know who Ip man was if it weren't for Bruce's close association with him. Besides, the two names were practically synonymous with each other (imagine making a John Woo biopic without the appearance of a Chow Yun-fat character). When Ip Man 2 finally made its way to theaters in 2010, the audience was treated to a nice surprise during the last few minutes of the movie: A digit old version of Bruce, played by Jiang Dai-Yan. Depending on how big of a Bruce Lee fan you are – and depending if you were expecting him or not – the cameo is worthy of goose bumps.

To date, Ip Man 2 was the first and only acting gig for Jiang. There are a number of premier/press conference photos of him performing kung fu stances in front of cast and crew, so this establishes that he's had some martial arts training. What's next for him? Only time will tell.

MASON LEE

Acclaimed director Ang Lee (Crouching Tiger, Hidden Dragon) will soon direct Bruce Lee, an upcoming biopic for Sony's 3000 Pictures. The filmmaker's son, Taiwanese-American actor Mason Lee, who is perhaps best known for his roles in 2011's The Hangover Part II and 2017's Legend of the Demon Cat, will be the latest actor who will be playing the iconic martial arts superstar.

Very little is known about Mason's martial arts ability, but according to People Magazine, he has been secretly "training" for the last 3 years in preparation for the role.

Ang Lee's Bruce Lee will be the first feature-length biopic, since Dragon: The Bruce Lee Story, that is officially co-signed by the Bruce Lee Estate, so it'll be interesting to see the final product, especially given the estate's negative

reaction to how Bruce was portrayed in both Birth of the Dragon and Once Upon A Time in Hollywood.

Whatever the case, we're hoping the film will be a solid Bruce Lee biopic and we look forward to Mason Lee's take on Bruce.

BRUCE LEE'S FILM & TV CAREER

Prior to "The Big Boss"
The Lowdown
By Simon Pritchard

Bruce - The actor

Bruce was born on the 27th November 1940 in San Francisco USA. His father, a Chinese opera star, moved the family back to Hong Kong in 1941 and introduced Bruce to acting. Bruce's first screen appearance was an infant in Golden Gate Girl also in 1941.

Bruce grew up in the film industry and was always primarily an actor that trained in Martial Arts. Bruce left for America in 1959 and eventually starred in 24 films between 1941 and 1960. Bruce attended University of Washington and opened a Gung-Fu school in Seattle. In 1966 Bruce moved to Los Angeles to further his acting career and got his first break as Kato, the sidekick, in the Green Hornet.

Bruce stared in nine TV shows between 1966 and 1971 where he then left of Hong Kong and star in The Big Boss. As well as acting, Bruce got his first experience behind the camera working as an Action Director on three films between 1968 and 1970. In 1969 Bruce was the Action Director on "Marlowe" where he managed to be in two scenes. This is where he met James Garner who later became a one of Bruce's students. The experience Bruce gained behind the camera in America was later shown in his own films, The Way of The Dragon and in the uncompleted Game of Death.

We include a Crib Sheet of all Bruce's work prior to 1971. If you manage to complete this list, in any format, from 35mm film to YouTube links; we would love to hear from you!

Bruce - The TV Shows

Bruce starred in nine TV shows between 1966 and 1971. Eastern Heroes has previously written about some of these shows but now is the time to fill the gaps to provide the most up-to-date information known so far.

*Bruce has appeared in interviews that are not listed here due to lack of information we have left them out, hopefully we will review this in a future issue as more information is gathered

1966

Where the Action Is

This episode first aired on the 1st September 1966 and ran for 30 minutes. This was a music based talent show on ABC hosted By Dick Clark and this episode had music from:

Sandy Posey – "Throw Caution to the Wind" and "Born a Woman".

The Knickerbockers - "Wild Thing" and "Tired of Waiting"

Steve Alaimo - "Um Um Um Um"

Paul Revere and the Raiders - "Take a Look at Yourself"

Bruce Lee cameoed as one of the dancers to the acts which was also shown in the fictionalised account of Bruce's life, The Dragon, staring Jason Scott Lee (1993).

The Green Hornet

Riding on the pop cultural wave of the late 1960's, Green Hornet was a character that first appeared in a radio show in 1936 and was created by the same man as The Lone Ranger. Funnily, in the storyline, The Green Hornet is actually the Lone Ranger's grand-nephew. Bruce played the sidekick Kato and showcased his martial arts ability for the first time on TV.

The Green Hornet was cancelled in 1967 and it's failure has been said to be down to the characters playing it "straight" and was not as camp as other shows at the time such as the most successful TV show, Batman.

For more information on the Green Hornet, please refer to "Eastern Heroes Bruce Lee Issue No 3 Green Hornet Special" available now.

1967 - Batman

Batman had a lot of cameos and in three episodes, "The Spell of Tut", "A Piece of the Action" and "Batman's Satisfaction", Van Williams and Bruce Lee stared as The Green Hornet and Kato in which Bruce

the Boy Wonder…. Jason McNeil reviews these episodes within "Eastern Heroes Bruce Lee Issue No 3 Green Hornet Special" in "Robin Vs Kato – Behind the Scenes of the Battle of the Sidekicks"

Ironside – "Tagged for Murder"

Season One Episode Seven first aired on the 26th October 1967 and ran for an hour. In this episode Ironside investigates an accidental electrocution that Ed thinks is a murder. Ed finds a pattern of murder

within a Swiss bank account. This leads to them discovering a group of WWII veterans have stored loot from a bank heist during the war.

Bruce Lee Plays Leon Soo, a son of a deceased Soldier and Instructor of Karate in an Aikido to Judo Martial Arts school. Bruce has a brief scene in this episode keeping him relevant on TV screens and the popularity of Ironside at the time, this isn't a bad little sequence.

1968 - Blondie - "Pick on a Bully Your Own Size"

Season One Episode thirteen first aired on the 9th January 1969 and ran for 24 minutes. Blonde revolves around a suburban couple raising two precocious children. The programme stars Patricia Harty as Blondie and Will Hutchins as her husband Dagwood Bumstead. The plot mixes typical sitcom tropes from home to work life. Blondie only ran for one season.

"Pick on a Bully Your Own Size" was the last episode aired where Bruce plays a Karate instructor Mr. Yoto. The show was abruptly cancelled during the filming for the next episode, "Run Buddy Run". Supposedly the cast and crew were all fired during their lunch break and asked to leave there and then.

We have located the script for Bruce's part in the episode. This episode with Bruce's appearance has never been located despite the attempts of many fans

Dressed in a karate outfit, the Japanese Instructor, Mr. Yoto, is demonstrating a series of strikes.

Yoto
Ahg!...Gha!...Keee!...Feee!
(stops and bows)
And now you try, Mr. Bumstead.
(looking around)
Mr. Bumsbead?

Mr. Yoto does a burn and goes to Mr. Bumstead, who we now see eating cookies and coffee from the free lunch cart. Mr. Bumstead is also in a karate robe outfit.

Yoto
Mr. Bumstead, you are not paying attention.

Mr. Bumstead
(with full mouth)
I'm sorry, Mr. Yoto. I didn't stop for dinner. I'll be with you in a minute.

Yoto
(angrily)

Not in a minute. NOW!

Yoto gives the wooden cart a karate slash with his hand, crumbling it and the food to the floor. Mr Bumstead is a bit shaken and looks petrified.
Mr. Bumstead
C-can I swallow what's in my mouth?

Yoto
Quickly!

Mr. Bumstead begins to vigorously chew the cookie left in his mouth, but can't manage to swallow it and has to chew again; another attempt to swallow and again he has to chew. He finally gets it down.

Mr. Bumstead
Tasty cookies, but tough. What are they?

Yoto
Octopus fudge brownies.

Mr. Bumstead turns a colour.

Yoto
Now, we try. You do same thing I show you.

Yoto takes a karate stance. Mr. Bumstead takes the same stance. Yoto begins to move around the room, jumping back and forth, slashing the air with his hands and feet. Mr. Bumstead, right behind Yoto, awkwardly imitates his every motion.

Last scene

Mr. Bumstead slashing the air with his hands. Yoto nodding his approval but correcting the angle of one of Mr. Bumstead hands. Blondie answering the front door to admit an exhausted Mr. Bumstead.

Mr. Bumstead watches Yoto set up three thick planks of wood. Yoto then drives the side of his hand through the planks, breaking them in half. He gestures for Mr. Bumstead to try it next. Yoto sets up three planks of wood. Mr. Bumstead shakes his head and removes two of them. Yoto nods, annoyed.

Blondie goes to the front door and admits Mr. Bumstead. He gives her an exhausted kiss and a wave goodnight. When he waves, we see his right hand is heavily bandaged.

Mr. Bumstead is then seem doing a series of karate moves much more gracefully.

Yoto watches with a smile of pleasure………

1969 - Here comes the Brides - "Marriage Chinese Style"

This is an American Comedy Western which is loosely based on Asa Mercer that

ran for two seasons. Asa Mercer tried to import woman to Seattle from the East Coast to marry men, in 1860's, due to their shortage of women. Bruce stared in Season One Episode 25 "Marriage

Chinese Style" which first aired on the 9th April 1969. Bruce plays Lin and this is one of the only roles, unfortunately short and brief, where Bruce portrays his more sensitive side. This is a non-violent role where his arranged fiancée is saved by the one of the main protagonists, Jeremy. She now believes she belongs to Jeremy and is less interest in the man she is there to meet, Lin.

1969 - Marlow

Bruce Lee (Winslow Wong) had a very small role in the Marlowe (1969) film. He was cast as a strong-arm thug employed by the local mob. Despite his lack of time on the big screen, his screen presence shined with a few great lines including James garner goading him whilst on the ledge of a building saying "You're a little light on your feet Wislow! Are you sure you're not a little gay"! Bruce in a rage does his

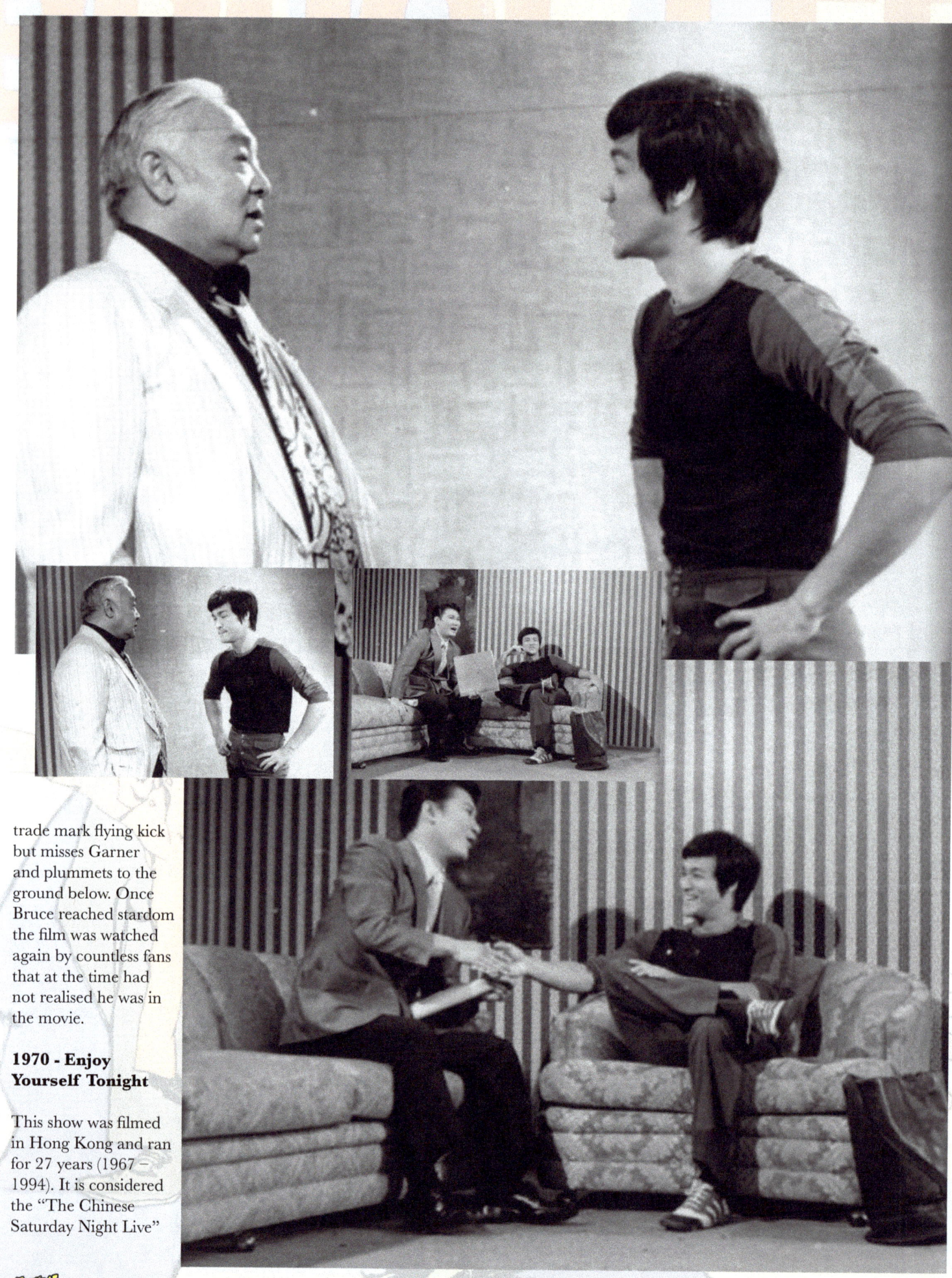

trade mark flying kick but misses Garner and plummets to the ground below. Once Bruce reached stardom the film was watched again by countless fans that at the time had not realised he was in the movie.

1970 - Enjoy Yourself Tonight

This show was filmed in Hong Kong and ran for 27 years (1967 – 1994). It is considered the "The Chinese Saturday Night Live" and one of world longest running life shows. Bruce demonstrated his moves and fitness, with one finger push-ups. The footage of this show can be seen below.

https://www.youtube.com/watch?v=8YdYHQDRcNM

1971 - Longstreet

This programme follows Mike Longstreet. An insurance investigator that is blinded by a bomb that also kills his wife. The pilot TV Movie "Longstreet" Sets the scene and was aired on the 23rd February 1971. It wasn't until the 16th September 1971 the first episode of the TV series aired called "The Way of the Intercepting Fist". This episode Longstreet meets an antique dealer called Li Tsung (Bruce) who he wishes to teach him how to defend himself.

Bruce stars in four episodes in Longstreet. By this time Bruce has developed his martial arts and philosophy which is shown throughout his performance. In hindsight, Bruce's ability had reached the limit of the side roles being offered in America and it was the right time to go to Hong Kong to progress into the lead role.

For more information on Longstreet, please refer to "Eastern Heroes Season one Episode 6" available now.

The Pierre Berton Show

This was a Canadian Talk Show that ran from 1962 to 1973. Pierre interviewed the notable people of the time from Malcolm X in 1965 to Lenny Bruce a year later in 1966. The Bruce Lee interview first aired on the 9th December 1971.

This is an exceptional interview that shows an insight into the person and martial artist, Bruce Lee, never seen before and unfortunately never seen since. Watch the full video here:

https://www.youtube.com/watch?v=uk1lzkH-e4U

HK-TVB Operation Relief Telethon June 24, 1972

On the 24th June [1972], HK-TVB television station broadcast a live fund raising event in aid of the victims of a devastating landslide that occurred the

1971 - Longstreet

week before on June 18th. The disaster, near Po Shan Road..., resulted in sixty seven fatalities, twenty serious injuries and two buildings completely destroyed. This was the result of unstable ground on a hillside following Typhoon Rose eleven months prior to the fatal incident. The show, which featured many of HK's celebrities of the time (including Bruce Lee doing demonstrations with the help of a 7 year old Brandon) went on to raise more than $8.5M for the relief fund. Locating the complete episode highlighting Bruce has forever remained a mystery to fans has his scenes are not included apart from some footage shot from the side lines on a movie camera.

THE LITTLE DRAGON TV & FILM APPEARANCES PRIOR TO 1971

Filmography

Year	Title	Chinese title
1941	Golden Gate Girl	金門女
1946	The Birth of Mankind	人类的诞生
1948	Wealth is Like a Dream	富貴浮雲
1949	Sai See in the Dream	夢裡西施
1949	The Story of Fan Lei-fa	(Unknown)
1950	The Kid	細路祥
1950	Blooms and Butterflies	(Unknown)
1951	Infancy	人之初
1951	A Myriad Homes	千萬人家
1951	Blame it on Father	父之過
1953	The Guiding Light	苦海明燈
1953	A Mother's Tears	慈母淚
1953	In the Face of Demolition	危樓春曉
1953	An Orphan's Tragedy	孤星血淚
1953	Orphan's Song	孤兒行
1955	Love	愛
1955	Love Part 2	愛(下集)
1955	We Owe It to Our Children	兒女債
1955	The Faithful Wife	(Unknown)
1956	The Wise Guys Who Fool Around	詐癲納福
1956	Too Late For Divorce	早知當初我唔嫁
1957	The Thunderstorm	雷雨
1957	Darling Girl	(Unknown)
1960	The Orphan	人海孤鴻

TV Shows

Year	Title	Chinese title
1966	The Green Hornet	青蜂俠
1966	Where the Action Is	(Unknown)
1967	Batman	蝙蝠俠
1967	Ironside	無敵鐵探
1968	Blondie	(Unknown)
1969	Here Comes the Brides	新娘駕到
1970	Enjoy Yourself Tonight	歡樂今宵
1971	Longstreet	血濺長街
1971	The Pierre Berton Show	(Unknown)

Action Director

Year	Title	Chinese title
1968	The Wrecking Crew	風流特務勇破迷魂陣
1969	Marlowe	酏聞諜血
1970	A Walk in the Spring Rain	春雨漫步

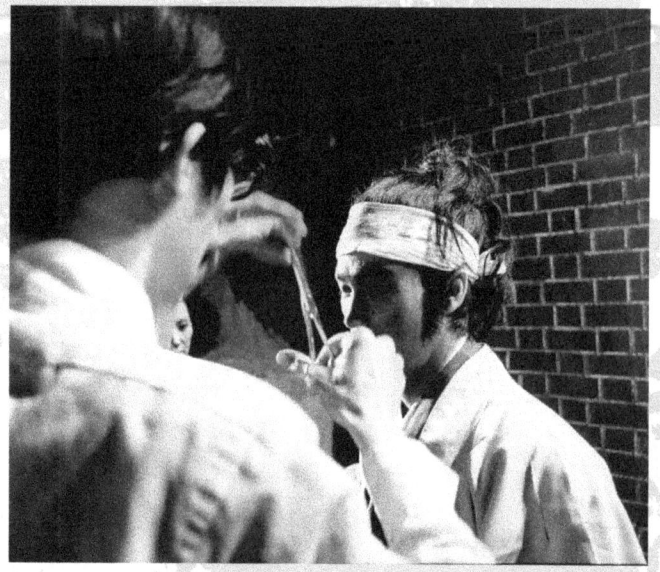

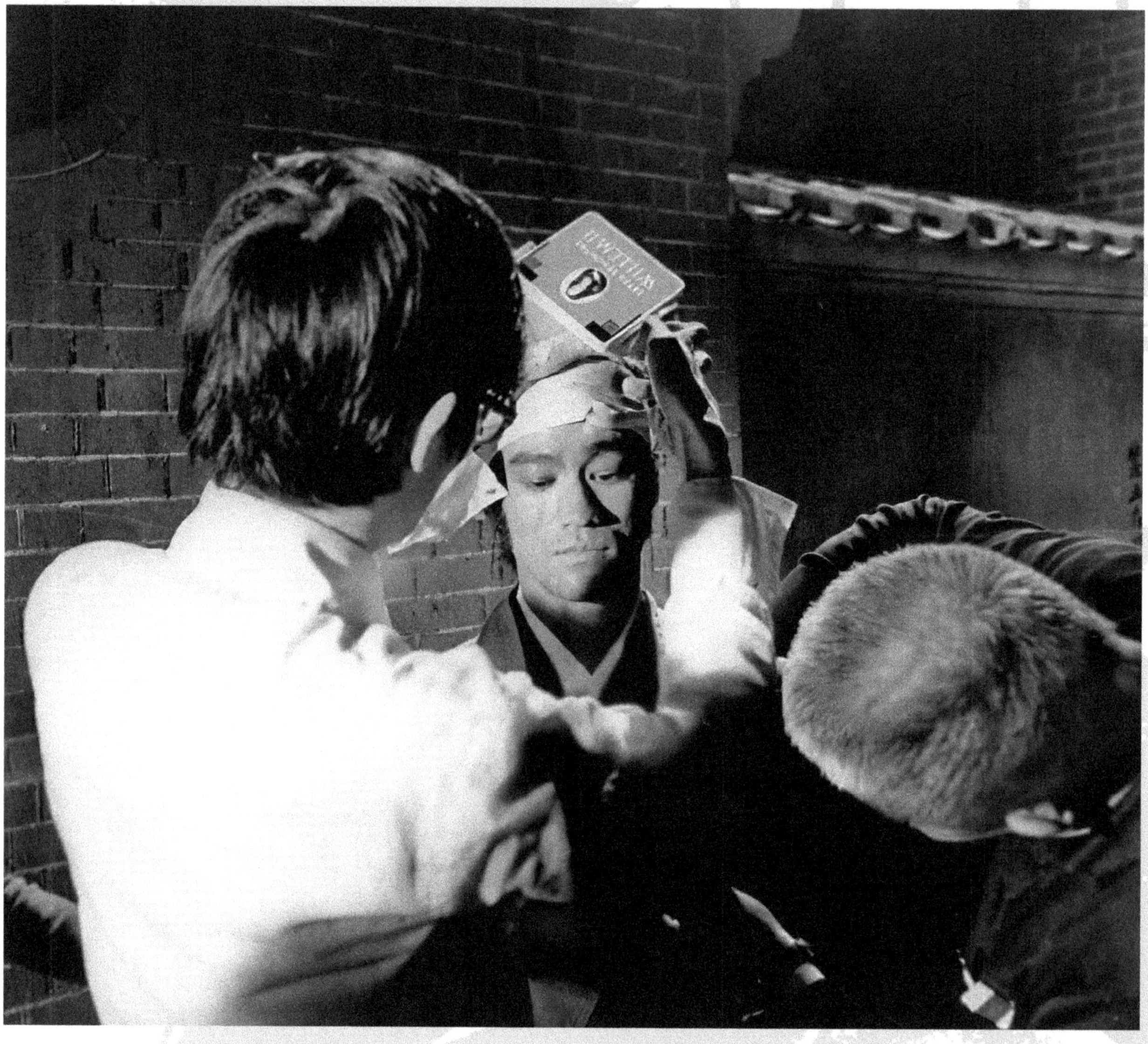

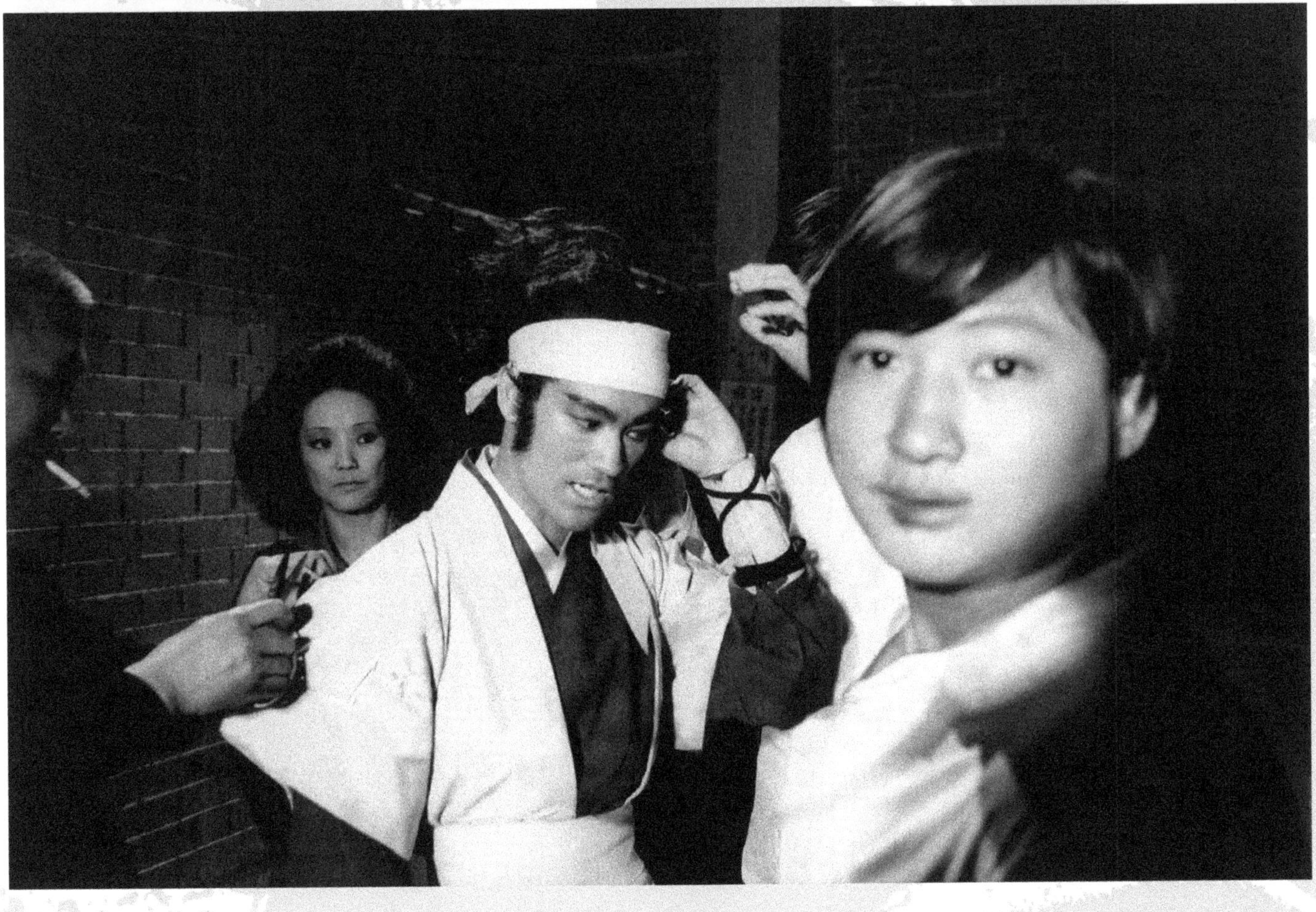

Bruce Lee Special #6 Page: 47

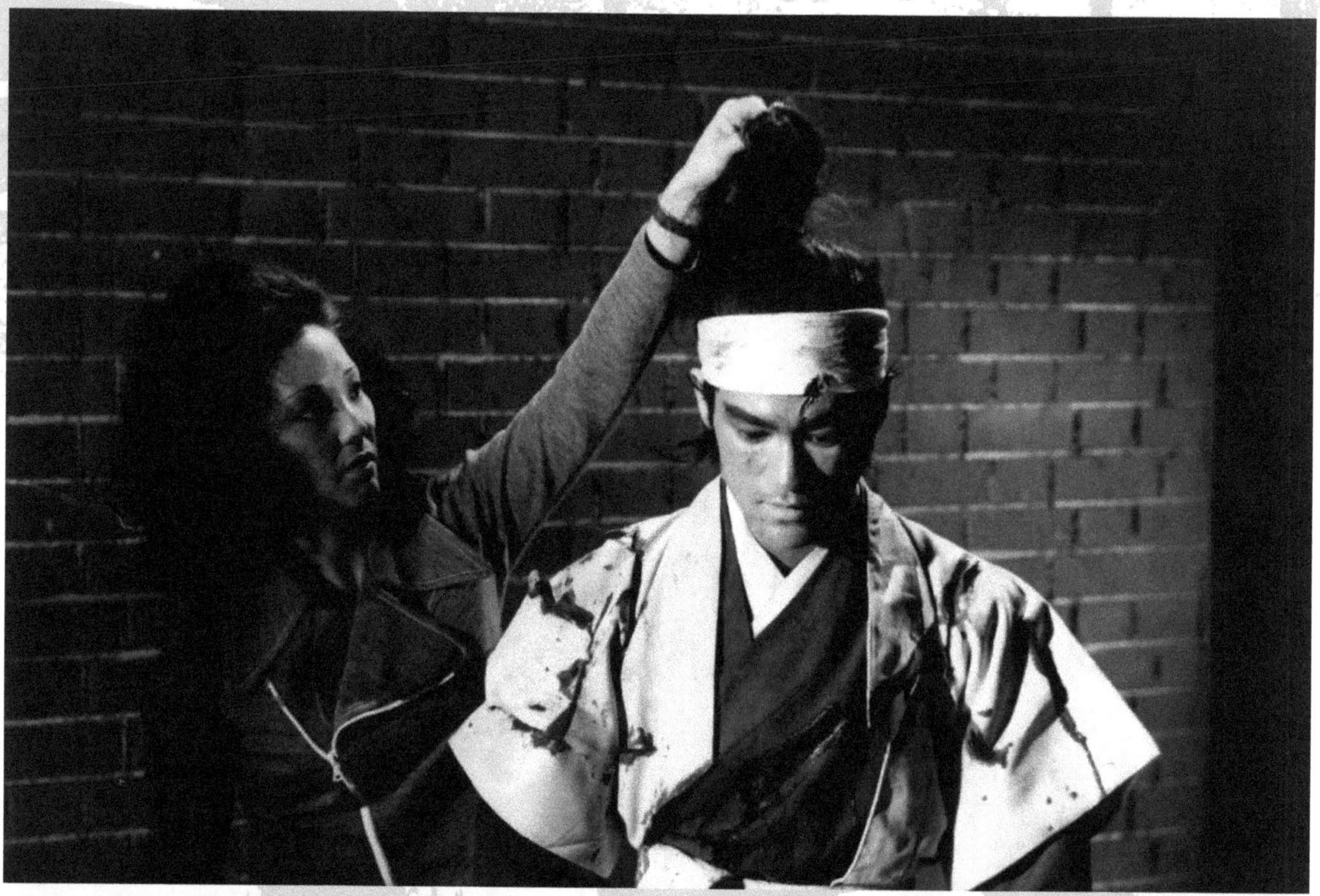

Bruce Lee Special #6 Page: 55

LIFE AFTER DEATH

The screening of "Game of Death Redux 2.0" on the BIG SCREEN! Rick Baker takes the red eye flight to New York to see that iconic yellow tracksuit on the big screen.

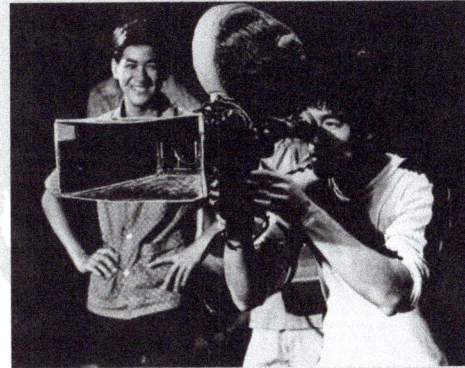

Normally on November the 5th I would be watching fireworks at some local event. But! In 2022 I was in the big apple to see Bruce Lee in all his heavenly glory, delivering fireworks in his own way, with multiple styles, and rapid nunchaku action delivering firecracker action in 30 minutes of pure art-house action. Alan Canvan's Redux 2.00 had its world premiere at "The Urban Action Showcase International Action Film Festival" in Times Square. This was UASC 10th anniversary and organiser Demetrius Angelo pulled out all the stops for this epic event packed with guest stars and exhibitions.

It was a privilege to watch Alan Canvan's new edit of Bruce Lee's "Game of Death" on the big screen, for me it was truly transformative experience. In just 30 minutes, Canvan was able to take what was originally just an uncompleted end of reel, and turn it into a contained, thought-provoking art-house film.

The editing work itself was simply breathtaking, Canvan was able to seamlessly integrate the new footage in a way that felt natural and enhanced the overall viewing experience. The pacing of the film was also spot on, with each scene flowing seamlessly into the next.

One of the other standout elements of Alan Canvan's edit is the way that John Barry's theme tune enhances the flow of the film. From the very first notes of the music, the audience is immediately drawn into the world of the film, and the music only becomes more powerful as the story progresses.

What I particularly love about Barry's theme tune is the way it perfectly captures the tone of the film. The music is both epic and emotional, perfectly complementing

李小龍

the high-stakes action and the deeper themes present in the film. It's a true masterpiece of film scoring.

But beyond just setting the mood, the music also serves to drive the narrative forward. The way the themes are woven into the different scenes and sequences helps to bring a sense of cohesion to the film, making it feel like a cohesive whole rather than a series of disparate events.

Overall, John Barry's theme tune for Bruce Lee's Game of Death is a true work of art that helps to elevate Alan Canvan's edit to new heights. It's a perfect example of how music can enhance the flow and impact of a film.

What also impressed me was the way that Canvan was able to elevate the themes of the original film. Through his editing, he was able to bring out the deeper meanings

and messages that were not present in the original footage, making for a truly enriching viewing experience.

There are a few reasons why seeing Bruce Lee's Game of Death on the big cinema screen is the ultimate way to fully appreciate it.

First and foremost, the larger screen size allows you to fully immerse yourself in the world of the film. The stunning cinematography and action sequences are given the space they deserve, making

it easy to get lost in the story and fully experience the film.

Another advantage of seeing the film on the big screen is the superior sound quality. The thumping soundtrack and intense sound effects are given a new level of depth and power when heard through a high-quality cinema sound system. This further enhances the overall viewing experience and helps to bring the film to life in a way that simply isn't possible on a smaller screen.

Finally, there's just something special about the communal experience of watching a film in a cinema. Being surrounded by other fans of the film and experiencing it together adds an extra level of excitement and enjoyment to the viewing experience. I was so happy that

I made the Journey, taking me back to the days when the only way I could see a Bruce Lee film was on the big screen, and it's those memories that I always reflect on when discussing one of Bruce's movies. Afterwards I, Ric Meyers and Alan did a panel chat which was the perfect way to educate the audience on some of the finer details that Bruce was trying to achieve within the Pagoda scenes. I hope Alan has the chance to do further screenings so that Bruce Lee fans can experience his Redux 2.0 in the same way I did and fully appreciate what he achieved with this edit. In summary - Alan Canvan's Game of Death Redux movie is a masterpiece of editing and filmmaking, seamlessly integrating new footage and special effects to elevate the themes and messages of the original film and create a truly enriching viewing experience.

GAME OF DEATH REDUX 2.0

BRUCE LEE: THE AUSTRIAN CONNECTION

By Peter Geissler

Being a rather small country, Austria movie distributors have always relied on material from Germany. Lobby cards, movie posters, all these are produced in our neighbor country. There is only a handful of genuine Austrian collectibles.

But before these are presented, let's take a short look on the Austrian cinema release history. To better understand it, here are the German movie titles for the Bruce Lee movies.

• Der Dritte im Hinterhalt (The Third in Ambush) = Marlowe

• Die Todesfaust des Cheng Li (The Death Fist of Cheng Li) = The Big Boss

• Todesgrüsse aus Shanghai (Death Greetings from Shanghai) = Fist of Fury

• Die Todeskralle schlägt wieder zu (The Death Claw Strikes Again) = Way of the Dragon

• Der Mann mit der Todeskralle (The Man with the Death Claw) = Enter the Dragon

• Das Geheimnis der grünen Hornisse (The Secret of the Green Hornet) = The Green Hornet

• Der gelbe Taifun (The Yellow Typhoon) = Fury of the Dragon

• Mein letzter Kampf (My Last Fight) = Game of Death

I have invested quite some time checking the relase dates of the Bruce Lee movies in the internet archive of the Austrian „Arbeiter Zeitung" (Workers Newspaper), which unfortunately is no longer online. And these are the results of my search.

• "Der Dritte im Hinterhalt": no exact release date available, Germany: Sept. 19th, 1969

• It was rather difficult to find the first screening of „Die Todesfaust des Cheng Li". The IMDB (Internet Movie Data Base) states the German release date as April 4th, 1973. So my seach began on this date. The first mention of the movie in Austria was on March 8th, 1974. It was shown in a small venue, the „Zentrum Kino", running there for two days. Then there is another screening, on March 13th, 1974, in the „Weltbild Kino". The movie shows up at various later dates but had no general release, contrary to all the other Bruce Lee films.

Kurier, March 13th, 1974 (excerpt from the movie program page)

• "Todesgrüsse aus Shanghai": Sept. 9th, 1973. Shown in two cinemas: „Kärntner Kino" and „Panorama Kino".

• "Der Mann mit der Todeskralle" April 26th, 1974 (opened in five cinemas: Elite Kino, Kärntner Kino, Panorama Kino, Maria-Theresien Kino, Kolosseum Kin

Kronen Zeitung, April 26th, 1974

The caption says: „The first ‚Eastern' from Hollywood that shows action in unprecedented perfection!"

• "Das Geheimnis der grünen Hornisse": Aug. 15th, 1975, „Kruger Kino"

Kurier, Aug. 22nd, 1975; „2. W." = 2nd week

• "Die Todeskralle schlägt wieder zu": Sept. 11th, 1975, „Apollo Kino"

Kurier, Sept. 12th 1975

„Never shown to us before! Bruce Lee: My best movie."

(Caption from the German paperboard mat.)

Generally, movies in Austria premiere on a Friday. As an exception to this rule, „Die Todeskralle schlägt wieder zu" was first shown on a Thursday.

• "Der gelbe Taifun": Mai 19th, 1976, „Kreuz Kino", Haydn Kino", „Auge Gottes"

This date is quite uncertain. May 19th was a Wednesday, so it would be a rather special premiere date. The IMDB states June 1976 as the release date, which is definitely wrong. An educated guess would be May 14th, a Friday. This is based on the confirmed information that the movie was no longer shown in the „Kreuz Kino" on Friday, May 21st.

Kronen Zeitung, May, 19th, 1976 (Caption: „New, genuine!")

KREUZ ½11, ½1, ½3, ½5, ½7, ½9. NEU, ECHT! Bruce Lee: DER GELBE TAIFUN

• "Mein letzter Kampf": May 26th, 1978: „Tabor Kino", „Apollo Kino". Again, Bruce breaks the rule and premieres on a Thursday.

Kronen Zeitung, May 25th, 1978
Kurier, May 26th, 1978

Caption: Finally it is here The last, real super movie of Bruce Lee finally authorized by the widow.

Caption: His new and last authentic movie, The real Bruce Lee

Austrian movie programs have a long history. The longest-running series is „Neues Filmprogramm" (New Movie Program). Founded in 1956, the series is still in print and sports a massive 14.800+ issues.

Programs measure 24 x 16 cm and have four pages. They feature pictures from the movie as well as information about the company, the filmcrew, actors and a synopsys of the plot.

With the exeption of „Die Todesfaust des Cheng Li", „Neues Filmprogramm" issued a program for every Bruce Lee movie at the time of it's release. The programs are rather easily available, with the execption of „Todesgrüsse aus Shanghai", which is quite rare.

Marlowe

Fist of Fury

Enter the Dragon

Enter the Dragon (Variant)

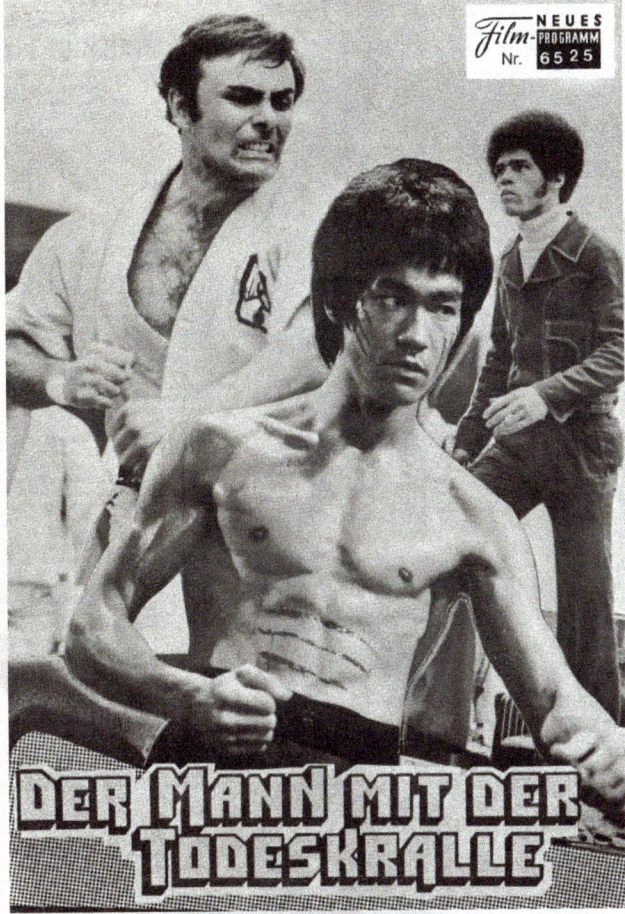

The Green Hornet

The Way of The Dragon

Fury of the Dragon

Game of Death

In February 2019, the current publisher of the „Neues Filmprogramm", Druck 3400 of Vienna, Austria, issued a program for „Die Todesfaust des Cheng Li". The program is part of a special series, „Filmindex", which concentrates on movies that had no program at the time of their release.

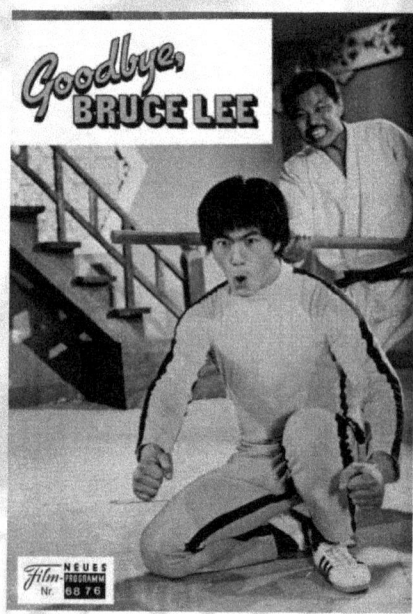

The Wrecking Crew — Super Dragon — Goodbye Bruce Lee - His Last Game of Death

A couple of Bruce-Lee-related movie programs, issued by „Neues Filmprogramm"

The Big Boss

Bruce Lee and I

The Unicorm Palm

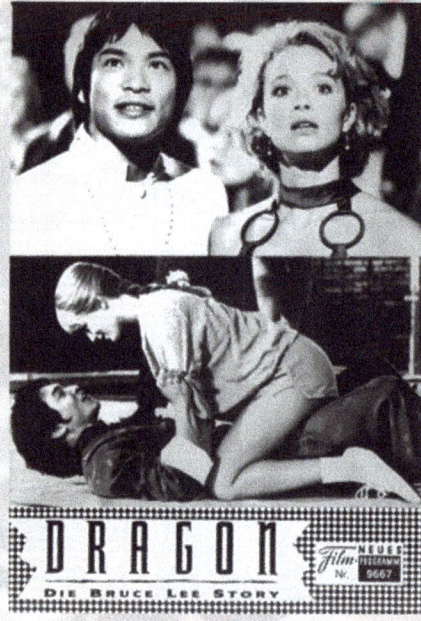
Dragon: The Bruce Lee Story

As I have stated before, most of the movie material used in Austria comes from Germany. With an outstanding exception!

By accident I stumbled over the (and I'm definitely not exaggerating) rarest Austrian collectible. Offered on an Austrian sales platform (willhaben.at) I found two banner-like movie posters for „Der Mann mit der Todeskralle" and „Der gelbe Taifun". The posters were produced in Vienna for the Austrian market. They measure 68 x 31 cm and were printed in Vienna. There are posters of this style for many other movies but they are extremly hard to find.

The guy who sold the posters obviously had no idea of what he had in hands! 15 Euro for the „Der gelbe Taifun" and a ridiculous 25 Euro for „Der Mann mit der Todeskralle"!

Bruce Lee: HE was and remains the GREATEST! The best Kung Fu Fighter of the world in an adventure full of action and – KARATE

The first „China-Movie" from Hollywood, a red hot action charge which can't be compared to anything! Thanks to Thomas Gross for mailing me a picture of another poster which unfortunately is not in my possession.

Bruce Lee in a movie full of excitement, action and KARATE

It is pretty safe to say that there is also a banner for „Mein letzter Kampf". There is a picture of an entrance to a cinema in Vienna in which you can see posters of „Mein letzter Kampf". The picture is a bit blurred but I'm quite sure that I spotted a banner for the movie. The search is on!

Peter Geissler, Vienna, Austria

The now truly iconic Yellow Jumpsuit that Bruce Lee wore for the scenes he shot for the Pagoda sequence in Game of Death has become of of Cinema's most instantly recognisable costumes, forever cemented in our memories of Bruce Lee and now having transcended to an almost symbiotic relationship with the Star. No other outfit that Bruce wore in any of his movies has achieved quite the same level of power nor the cinematic currency which that Yellow suit with the single Black stripe down the side has achieved. The staggering amount of appearances in other media which the outfit has gone on to feature in, a testament not just to Bruce Lee's incredible star power and influence on countless generations of filmmakers, but to the sheer visual impact that the suit commands.

I've heard countless rumours over the years as to the origins of the suit itself, ranging from Bruce being inspired by a skiing trip with film Director Roman Polanski when Lee wore a similar coloured ski suit (this is fairly likely, the two were very close friends and did take a few vacations together) through to tales that the original choice for the movie was for a black suit with a yellow stripe which Lee opted to change around just before shooting the Pagoda sequence footage so that Kareem Abdul-Jabbar's footprint would be more visible (this seems less likely).

I've already looked at the various Blu-ray editions of the original Game of Death movie (and the re-edited Pagoda sequence which better serves to present Bruce's True vision for the film) in this section back in the first Bruce Lee Special Issue, so this time around I'd like to dive into some of the most notable editions of movies that showcase and celebrate the suit in all it's glory and help continue to cement it's place as one of the all time greatest Movie Costumes…

I was actually lucky enough to see the original suit Lee wore at the Bruce Lee Kung Fu, Art Life Exhibition held at the Hong Kong Heritage Centre, we were able to sneakily grab a photo of the suit which I have included here too, it was taking pride of place in a reconstruction of part of the Game of Death pagoda set, it is still on site and available to view currently as part of the Museum's current A Man Beyond the Ordinary: Bruce Lee exhibition for anyone visiting HK anytime soon.

For now though, Grab your Yellow Nunchucks and your Onitsuka Tiger Sneakers and let's begin….

1) Kill Bill Volume 1 - 2003
   Dir - Quentin Tarantino
   Japanese UNCUT DVD Boxset

Probably the reference most mainstream Western Audiences are most familiar with, even to the extent that I've heard some folks frustratingly referring to Bruce's Outfit in Game of Death as his 'Kill Bill' clothing. Tarantino leaned hard into Game of Death in the many, many influences he fused into the two Kill Bill movies. Here using the Yellow and Black stripe colour scheme across most of the movies marketing and promotional materials and also decking Uma Thurman's Bride character out in a (Two Piece) tribute to the original Jumpsuit for the spectacular House of Blue Leaves sequence in Kill Bill Pt1. I'm assuming everyone reading this will be familiar with the two movies, The Bride left for dead by the titular Bill, her former employer along with her fellow cohorts and after awakening from a coma starts off on a long road of revenge, working her way through dispatching the other Assassins she had previously worked alongside, marking them off a list one by one until she can eventually….Kill Bill.

The movie is widely available on Blu-ray but in it's censored form, the key action sequence in the House of Blue Leaves from the first movie drops into Black and White for much of the battle.
I would recommend tracking down the UNCUT Japanese DVD edition of the film, which retains full colour for the entire sequence in all its Blood Drenched, limb severing, Kung Fu / Samurai mashup glory. No official plans to release the Uncut version on Blu-ray so far, The Japanese DVD editions remain the best way to see the movies in their rawest form so far and if you can find the Boxset I've shown here, you even get a little Bearbrick Figure sporting the Yellow and Black suit, very cool indeed.

2) Dynamo - 1978
   Dir - Hua Shan / Haw I Hung
   Pearl River BluRay/ DVD

One of the very best Ho Chung-tao aka Bruce Li Bruceploitation movies, both in terms of story and action, It features archive footage of HK from during Lee's funeral, and in a pretty meta narrative for one of these movies… Bruce Li is recruited within the movie by an

unscrupulous advertising company seeking to capitalise on Bruce Lee's untimely death and the perceived need for a new Martial Arts star to be found to fill his shoes. Talk about art imitating life imitating art! Bruce Li's Taxi Driver Lee Tien-yee is hired by Mary Hon's Ad Agency and the agency pull out every trick to make Li into an overnight sensation. Shaw Brother's veterans Ku Feng and Lee Hoi San both co-star, Ku Feng especially is on very fine form here as Li's chain smoking, sassy Sifu. Bruce Li dons the famous Yellow and Black suit (and a white and red alternate) in the film. And looks the part far more than most. The soundtrack is also pretty damn funky. Directed by another Shaw Brothers veteran, Hua Shan (here credited as Haw I Hung), the director of the Shaw Brothers take on Ultraman, The Super Infra-man, who here manages to balance a great mix of Action along with way more attention given to character and story than was often paid by the bulk of the Bruceploitation movies.

There is a fantastic Blu-ray/DVD combo edition of the movie available from relatively new label Pearl River, the label started by the wonderful Bruceploitation Podcast The Clones Cast host and creator Micheal Worth. It's really a fantastic release, with a commentary track by Worth and some wonderful cover art by Arrow Video regular Ian McEwan along with featurettes on the 2K restoration created for the discs from the original negative as well as a feature on the creation of McEwan's artwork. Highly recommended! If you only pick up one Bruceploitation flick, make it this one, It's one of the movies Bruce Li is most proud of from his career, and it's not hard to see why.

You can also check out Michael Worth's wonderful interview with Bruce Li which appeared in Eastern Heroes Issues 2+3 as well as his fantastic podcast The Clone Cast, which you can find on Spotify, Apple Podcasts and Direct via the Screen Mayhem Website.

3) **Enter The Game of Death - 1978**
   German Title - Das Spiel Des Todes
   Dir - Lee Tso-nam
   The Vengeance Pack Mediabook
   Blu-ray / DVD

Another of the best Bruceploitation movies. This time with Wong Kin-lung aka Bruce Le (who co-incidentally acted in Hua Shan's Super Infra-man) stepping up to the plate and also co-starring the mighty Bolo Yeung in a film with much more of a narrative tribute/homage/rip-off of Game of Death than many other movies that tried to cash in on Lee's legacy. Originally released under the title Cross Hands Martial Arts the film sees Bruce Le being hired to retrieve a mysterious document from the 'Tower of Death'. It's a fairly insane movie all in all, jam packed with far more action than plot, so it can be a confusing watch first time around, but it's great fun, funky as hell and actually holds a higher rating online than Bruce Lee's original Game of Death. Directed with gusto by Lee Tso-nam who also directed Fist of Fury II (itself a far more effective sequel to the original than Lo Wei's Jackie Chan starring New Fist of Fury).

This is another Bruceploitation movie that we're lucky enough to have a pretty fantastic Blu-ray release for, this time around from the wonderful maniacs The Vengeance Pack in Germany.
It's a very English friendly release, with English and German audio options and TVP made the very wise move of getting the incredibly talented Kung Fu Bob O'Brien to make a cover for the release (one of three options available) it comes as a limited edition Bluray as well as a

equally limited edition Blu-ray/DVD Mediabook, which if you're lucky also comes with a poster inside.

4) **Shaolin Soccer - 2001**
   Dir - Stephen Chow
   Korean Bluray

The first of Stephen Chow's comedies to really break internationally after Miramax picked up the international rights to the film and released it pretty heavily in the US (Optimum Asia originally put it out on DVD here in the UK). Stephen Chow's

excellent comedy is as much about martial arts as it is about football. Chow's Shaolin disciple Sing joining up with his regular collaborator (and sadly recently deceased) Ng Man-Tat's Golden Leg Fung to form a Soccer team to go up against Fung's double crossing former teammate Tse Yin (Father of Raging Fire star Nicholas Tse). The comedy still holds up well and you can see Chow laying the ground work for much of the same style of visual effects infused set pieces that he would later master in Kung Fu Hustle.

It's place on this list is secured by the wonderful Bruce Lee impression in the movie by the teams goalkeeper 'Empty Hand' played with relish by the amazing Danny Chan Kwok-kwan, sporting the Yellow jumpsuit along with a handful of signature Bruce moves.

Again, another title pretty widely available on Blu-ray and DVD, but I've opted to highlight the wonderful Korean edition of the film, available via Nova Media, mostly because it comes in a rather spiffy Yellow Slipcase. It has a few extra features on it, some short behind the scenes featurettes, a music video and trailers, though sadly no English subs on the extras
(there is on the main feature though).
Go Kick some Grass!

5) High Risk AkA Meltdown - 1995
Dir - Wong Jing
Japanese Import Bluray / Korean DVD

The last one on the list is also the trickiest to track down on Blu-ray, Wong Jing's parody of Die Hard mixed with Speed starring Jet Li and co-starring Jackie Cheung here playing a vain, rather inept Movie Star famous for doing his own stunts who in reality relies heavily on Jet Li who reluctantly acts as his bodyguard and secret stunt double. Cheung's character wears the Yellow suit in a couple of key scenes in the movie. This often crops up to stream on Amazon, but is available on Blu-ray by way of a Japanese Import, and I wouldn't be too surprised if the good folks over at 88 films or Eureka didn't pick this one up for a UK release at some point. It's a pretty silly movie overall but the action is well staged thanks to the presence of Cory Yuen on choreography duties, and the ever watchable, considerable talents of Jet Li.

The Japanese Blu-ray is pretty bare bones and is not English friendly, there are English subtitled DVD's available, either via the old UK Region2 release or the Korean Region3 release.

And just as we were going to print, Shamrock Media in Germany have announced they will be releasing 3 separate Cover editions of High Risk as a Blu-Ray / DVD Mediabook.
No price or release date known as yet, but the release will definitely be English Friendly.
That's already looking like it'll be the best edition of the movie to track down for those keen to add it to their collection.

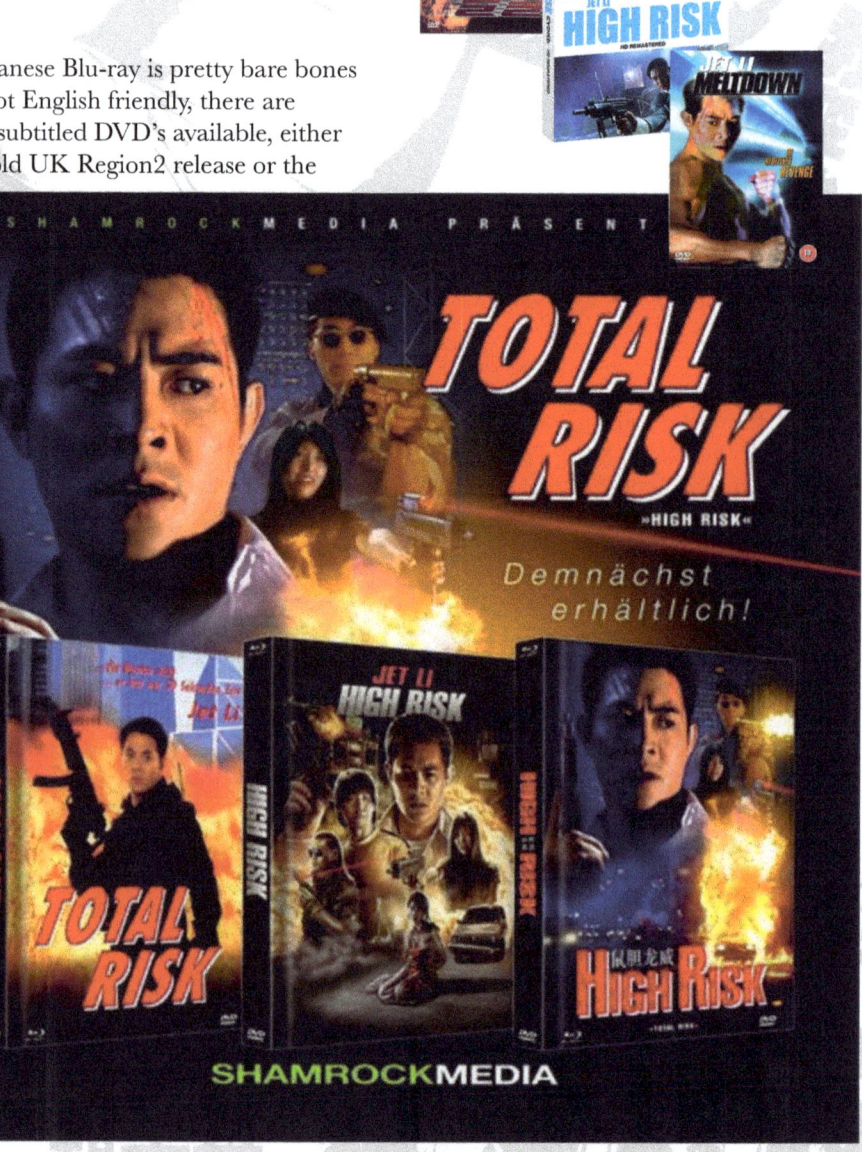

Honorable Mentions..

The true Die Hard Jackie Chan fans amongst us, already maybe aggrieved that I've included Wong Jing's rather thinly veiled and somewhat scathing attack on JC movie 'High Risk' on this list, may also be questioning why I didn't include The Yellow and Black North Face Jacket and Ski Trouser set JC wears in Police Story 4 aka First Strike, well, A) it's not technically the same Jumpsuit, more of a tip of the hat to the colour scheme and B) Jackie already actually featured a far more fitting tribute to Game of Death in City Hunter which features a straight clip of the original film, specifically the scene with Bruce Vs Kareem Abdul-Jabbar inspiring Jackie in how to deal with two towering opponents in the Cruise Ship's cinema. (Incidentally this was The Film he made with Wong Jing which in turn led to their falling out and Jing going on to poke fun at Jackie in High Risk)

Speaking of Wong Jing, The suit was also used extensively in the promotional materials for Donnie Yen's 2020 Re-imagining of Enter The Fat Dragon, directed by Wong.

There are also more Video Game references to the classic outfit than I can include here without running to more pages than I'm allowed, but the main ones I usually think of are Marshall Law's alternate outfit in Tekken. Chie Satonaka's Persona in the JRPG Persona 4. In the fantastic Sleeping Dogs where it also appears as a unlockable outfit for main character Wei Shen and even randomly in the original The Last Of Us game, where it can be used as an alternative outfit for Ellie after completing the game at Survivor difficulty level. And as the third outfit choice for Jann Lee in Dead or Alive 4.

Countless cartoons and Anime shows have also referenced the suit over the years, maybe the most fun and unexpected one has to be Spongebob Squarepants, Sandy donned the suit in Karate Island, itself actually kinda a mashup tribute to Enter The Dragon and Game of Death narratively as well as visually.

These are by no means ALL of the various references and uses of the outfit over the years these are just a few of my favourites. I'm very sure we've not seen the last of Bruce's most infamous outfit making an appearance in movies, games and comics!

Huge thanks to my good friend Jason from The Martial Arts Theater 3000 Youtube page for all his help with my Bruceploitation fact checking.

See you all in the next issue!

Written by Johnny 'The Fanatical Dragon' Burnett

You can find all my video previews of Eastern Heroes latest issues, Bluray reviews, Unboxings and more at: www.youtube.com/thefanaticaldragon

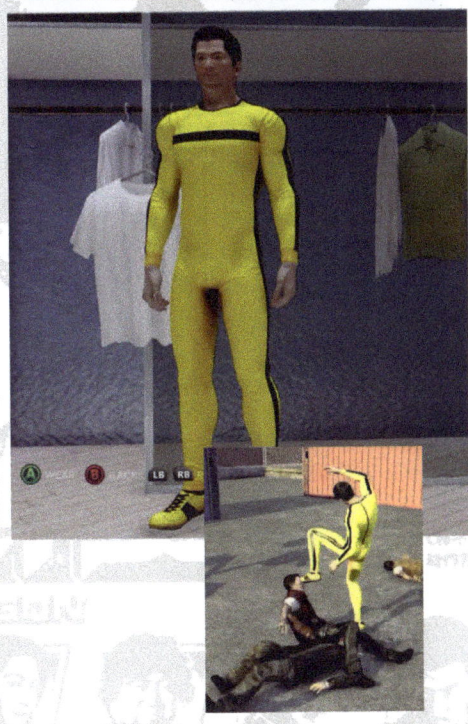

BE WATER MY FRIEND

Was Bruce's Death contributed by hyponatraemia?
By Rick Baker

Back in the 90s, Toby Russell and George Tan created probably one of the best documentaries as to the mystery behind Bruce lee's death with the documentary "DEATH BY MISADVENTURE". Tragically, he died six days before "Enter the Dragon" was to be released in Hong Kong. The mysterious circumstances of his death were a source of speculation for many who could not understand why a man at his peak suddenly passed away. Since the birth of the internet the rumours have continued from assassination to more recent finding that heat stroke could have been a possible cause. But for many, they still feel that foul play was at hand. It's very easy to be dragged down a rabbit hole of conspiracy theories. Personally I feel that medical science will always hold the truth, and I will never be convinced that his death was caused by any of the conspiracy that you can find on the many pages covering his death.

More recently an article appeared on the internet conducted by a group of research specialist that published a paper in the 2022 December edition of the clinical kidney journal. They stated that The legendary martial artist and actor known for saying, "Be water, my friend," may have consumed too much of it. At the time, his death was ruled the result of cerebral edema, or swelling of the brain, and almost 50 years later, a new study proposed that Lee's demise was caused by his "kidney's inability to excrete excess water."
Up to now, the cause of Bruce Lee's death is still unknown, although numerous hypotheses have been put forward, Tragically, the paper reads, before stating that while the average human brain weighs around three pounds, Lee's was reportedly closer to 3.5 pounds at the time of his death. According to

AU. 4566
1/42

DEPARTMENT OF SCIENTIFIC AND INDUSTRIAL RESEARCH

CHEMISTRY DIVISION

Telephone 699 199
Telegrams CHEMDIV, Petone

Private Bag,
Petone, New Zealand

31 August 1973

Dr R.R. Lycette,
Clinical Pathology Unit,
Queen Elizabeth Hospital,
Kowloon,
HONGKONG

Bruce LEE

Samples of blood and urine from the above deceased were received from you on 20 August 1973 for analysis for the presence of cannabis substances.

No detectable amounts of tetrahydro-cannabinol (THC) or cannabinol (CBN), the principal ingredients of cannabis, were detected in the blood.

I enclose a letter from Mr H.M. Stone, elaborating some detail of the analytical method for cannabis in blood.

(A.J. Ellis)
Director

...Encl.

IN THE CORONERS COURT
AT TSUEN WAN
EXHIBIT NO: 2B
DEATH ENQUIRY NO. 661/73(u)

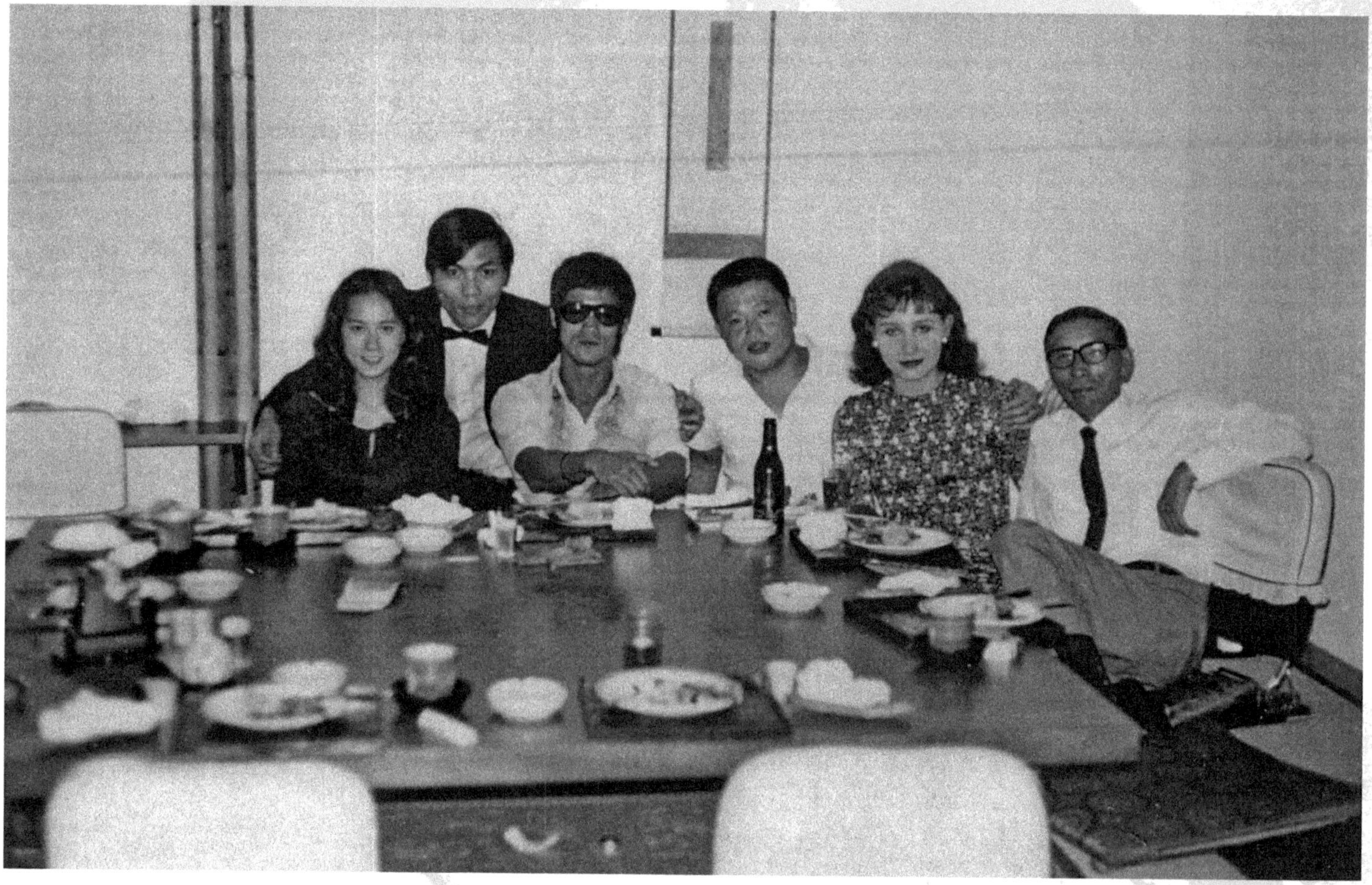

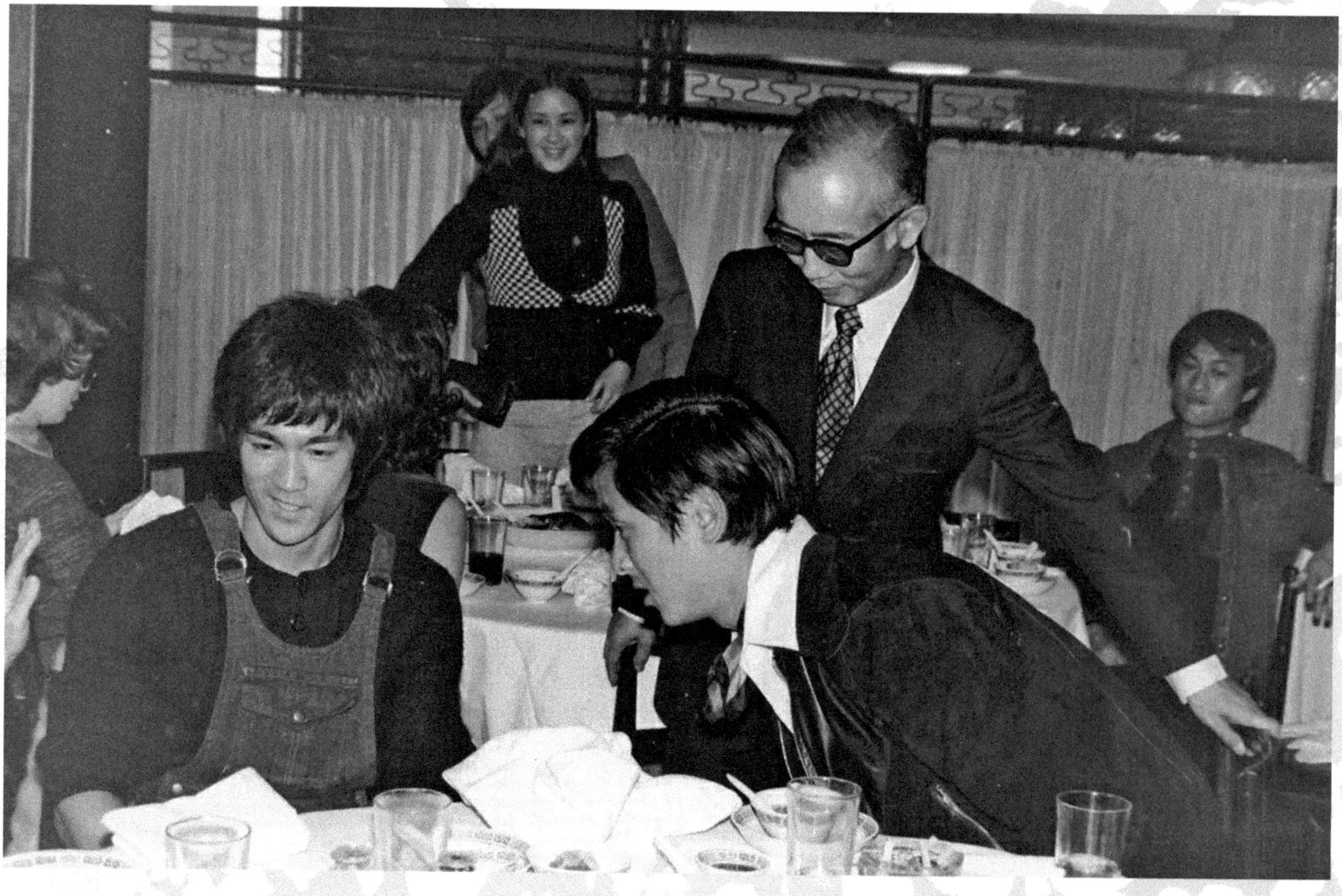

The following report concerns the post-mortem examination of Bruce Lee and includes certain other tests. The post mortem was witnessed by Drs. I. Filshie and K.T. Tham, and the microscopic sections were studied in collaboration with Dr. T.B. Teoh, Consultant Pathologist, i/c.

I take full responsibility for all the statements made and for the conclusions drawn.

The body of Bruce Lee was directly identified to me by his brother, Mr. Peter Lee. This identification was at the mortuary of the Queen Elizabeth Hospital, on 23rd July, 1973, at about 2.30 p.m.

Post Mortem and Tissue Report

The body is that of a well-built Chinese male of about 30 years of age and is 172 cm in length.

There are no external signs of injury. There is a small surgical incision on the inner aspect of the left ankle. There is a needle puncture mark on the front of the left chest, 5 cm from the mid-line and 11 cm vertically from the sternal notch. There is an old and healed linear scar (10 cm) situated in the right groin.

There are no recent or old needle marks, or unusual scars on the arms.

Central Nervous System

The scalp is free of bruising and the skull shows no evidence of fracture or injury, either recent, or old.

The brain shows a moderate degree of congestion of the surface vessels. The brain is very tense beneath the covering dura. The brain weighs 1,575 grams (normal for male up to 1,400 grams), and shows some tonsillar coning, but little uncinate groving - the former is evidence of brain swelling. The cerebral arteries are virtually free of atherosclerosis and have a normal pattern of distribution. A careful search of all vessels fails to reveal any evidence of aneurysm.

5200231 Pol. 154

ROYAL HONG KONG POLICE FORCE
STATEMENT / REPORT

Report No. KC/MRB/X6548/73 .... Kowloon City .... Station.
Name of informant/witness .... Dr. Peter WU Hin-ting .... age adult .... sex male .....
Address ...... Room 338, Tung Ying Building, Nathan Road, Kowloon ....
Occupation ...... Doctor
Nationality and dialect ....
Taken by .. Det. Insp. LAI Yuen-wing .... in ...... English .... language
at .... hours on ...... 17th August, 1973 ..... at (Place) ....
Interpreter ....

States:— I am as the above stated. I am a doctor. My qualifications are M.B., B.B. Hons. (H.K.) F.R.C.S. (Eng) M.R.C.P. (Edin.)

2. Mr. Bruce LEE was first seen by me in consultation with Doctor Don Langford in the afternoon of 10th May, 1973 in the Emergency Room of Baptist Hospital where he was admitted in coma.

3. The history was that he was in studio working that morning. He took some spagatti for lunch. Then he found to have vomited and collapsed in the toilet. He had had a siezure. On admission to Baptist Hospital he was apnoeic with rigidity in all limbs. Examination revealed that the pupils were pin-pointed and nonreactive. Fundi showed marked spasm of vessels. Respiration was periodic. Reflexes were depressed and plantar responses were negative.

4. After resuscitation and Mannitol therapy he gradually regained consciousness. Spontaneous respiration returned. Examination then revealed nystagmus to right and left and rotatory nystagmus was present. Blood culture was done and Haematological examination was carried out.

5. He was then transferred to St. Teresa's Hospital for further treatment. Blood chemistry: Na 154 mEq/L. K 4.8 mEq/L Chloride 97.44 mEq/L. Bicarbonate 20 mEq/L. Urea 92 mg/100 ml.

6. He became fully conscious and well orientated the next day. Nystagmus was still marked. Lumbar puncture was performed. Pressure 100 mm c.s.f. Fluid was clear and colourless W.B.C. 1/Cu. mm. R.B.C. 2/cu. mm. Protein 15 mg/100 ml. Sugar 73 mg/100 ml. Chloride 118 mEq/L. V.D.R.L. -ve.

7. Further investigation of bilateral carotid angiography was advised and scheduled for 14th May, 1973.

8. In view of the normal findings in the lumbar puncture Mr. LEE was interviewed along with his wife in his ward on 13th May, 1973 when he told me that he had taken a piece of Cannabis leaf before the onset of illness in studio on 10th May, 1973.

9. Mr. LEE requested to be discharged on the 13th May, 1973. He refused to take other kinds of test and he revealed that he would be leaving for the U.S.A. in a couple of weeks' time. He stated that he would have the test in the U.S.A.

10. My clinical diagnosis on Mr LEE were (1) Cerebral oedema, and (2) Poisoning by Cannabis suspected.

11. The above statements have been read by me and they are the truth to the best of my knowledge.

This form may be used to record reports (a) taken while Report Book is not available.

the researchers, Lee had "multiple risk factors for hyponatraemia"—extremely low sodium concentration in a person's blood. The condition may have been exacerbated by "chronic fluid intake," use of marijuana (which increases thirst), alcohol consumption, prescription drug intake, and a documented history of organ injuries. "In conclusion, we hypothesize that Bruce Lee died from a specific form of kidney dysfunction: the inability to excrete enough water to maintain water homeostasis, which is mainly a tubular function," the study states. "This may lead to hyponatraemia, cerebral oedema, and death within hours if excess water intake is not matched by water excretion in urine, which is in line with the timeline of Lee's demise." (Vanity Fair has reached out to a manager for Lee's daughter, Shannon, for comment about the study and its findings.)

"Given that hyponatraemia is frequent, as is found in up to 40% of hospitalized persons and may cause death due to excessive water ingestion even in young healthy persons," the researchers continue, "there is a need for a wider dissemination

of the concept that excessive water intake can kill." Despite this not being conclusive, I thought it made for a better explanation than some of the theories that have been put forward. Whatever the outcome we tragically lost a superstar that has yet to be replaced, but has left a legacy that has inspired millions and will continue to do so. I exclude a few of the pages of the official cause of death from the coroner's office

In memory of a once fluid man

WALL TO THE BALLS

(More or Less) True-ish Tales of Bob Wall's Martial Arts and Movie Star Badassery (According to Bob Wall)

By Jason McNeil

There is no doubt that Bob Wall led a pretty awesome life, was a world class martial artist, hobnobbed with the greats of chop socky cinema and appeared in some pretty seminal Kung-Fu flicks, including Enter the Dragon (where he quite famously and dramatically was on the receiving end of perhaps the most famous nut shot in history, courtesy of Bruce Lee, himself!) as well as Way of the Dragon, Game of Death and even Black Belt Jones.

And if you did dare to doubt his awesomeness for even a moment, Bob was always eager to remind anyone who would listen that he was the biggest, brightest and badassest in just about any room, dojo or Hong Kong TV studio!

Any conversation with Bob Wall would most definitely include him reminding you, multiple times, that he was a World Professional Martial Arts Champion (Retired), Martial Arts Movie Bad Guy, Best Buddies to both Bruce Lee and Chuck Norris, a World Traveller, etc., etc., etc.

Then, he would usually segue into increasingly unlikely and, frankly, pretty unbelievable stories about martial arts death matches in Hong Kong, then he'd remind you how much money he made in real estate, then he'd start ticking off names of Big Movie Stars whom he "had to" beat up for real, to "teach them a lesson" about what a badass Bob Wall was.

Then he'd call Enter the Dragon director Robert Clouse an asshole.

Then he'd remind you how rich he was again.

And so on......

Frankly, as anyone who ever interviewed Bob Wall will tell you, the hardest part about writing a Bob Wall piece wasn't the interview – it was the editing. Truth and reason and notions of "responsible journalism" would be screaming in one's ear while pecking away at the keyboard at 2 AM, while the deadline loomed, saying "No, you can't say that! That probably never happened, and you have no way to check! OK, it sounds like part or most of that may have actually happened, and its a cool story, but the end part is clearly a bunch of self-aggrandizing bullshit. There's no way that Bob and Bruce Lee actually went over to that guy's apartment and beat him up and ..... GAHHHHH! This is due in 6 hours!!!!!"

All that having been said....

We decided "What the hell?"

Let's let Bob Wall tell Bob Wall's Story, the

way Bob Wall wanted to - and often did - tell Bob Wall's story.

What follows, dear reader, are a collection of Bob Wall's best vignettes, remembrances and behind-the-scenes stories, just the way Bob Wall told them in an interview I helped put together in March 2013.

Whether or not what follows is all true, I cannot say. What I can say is that its all Bob, as Bob remembered it, or at least told everyone was how he remembered it, and maybe he even believed most or all of it – or at least some of it - himself.....

You be the judge.

Either way, sit back, relax and enjoy a heaping helping of Bob Wall – unedited, unfiltered and exactly the way Bob Wall wanted the stories about Bob Wall to be told.

HOW BOB WALL WAS CAST IN WAY OF THE DRAGON!

Bob: "Chuck Norris and I were 50/50 partners in a chain of schools. We had a large chain of schools. One of our largest schools – Torrance, California 1972 – and Chuck's on the phone, talking to Bruce. Bruce had called. So, he gets off the phone and he says 'I'm going to Rome! Then I'm going to Hong Kong to do a movie with Bruce!' And I'm like 'We're 50/50 partners, baby! You're not going without me!' So I paid my own way. So we're on the plane, getting ready to land in Rome, and Chuck said 'You know, the budget is real low, so they're going to be filming me when I'm getting off the plane. So he asks me if I could ask the person on the plane to 'Stop everybody for just half a minute so I can step off the plane and stop and look around.' So that shot in Way of the Dragon of Chuck arriving? That was Chuck arriving! That was the real plane! They couldn't afford it. So Bruce was there, set up. I'm the one that stopped people and said 'Hold on just for a minute, they're shooting out there.' He steps out and he does this deadly look around, we walk down the stairs, and Bruce says 'You're here! OK, you're in the movie! You get 75 a week and room and board!' 75 a week! That's how I got on.

HOW BOB WALL IS ENTIRELY RESPONSIBLE FOR THE COLUSSEUM FIGHT IN WAY OF THE DRAGON BECAUSE OF HIS MAFIA CONNECTIONS!

Bob: "I got us into the Colosseum, Which, was an amazing thing, because it was shut down. You couldn't get in there. But I'm married to a Sicilian, auspiciously. She made some calls and got us in there. I have some pictures of the Mafioso who got us in there with Bruce and Chuck and I."

WHY BOB WALL THOUGHT WAY OF THE DRAGON KIND OF SUCKED!

Bob: "To be honest with you, I did not like Way of the Dragon. I didn't like it while we were filming it, and I didn't like it after it came out. For me, it was almost an embarrassing film: country bumpkin goes to Rome and can't speak the language and.... What I loved about it was Bruce's skills. His martial arts skills and what he put on the screen. The fight scenes there are awesome! But, for me, I didn't like the story. The whole thing seemed dumb to me. But I thought 'Ehh, I'm here because of Bruce and I'm in a movie, so....' I was not then and am not now a big fan of Way of the Dragon. And yet, its one of the most awesome films, because its Bruce Lee at his only comedic best self. The only really comedic thing he did. So, for that reason, its very very good, but to me, it was no Enter the Dragon."

THAT TIME BOB WALL TRIED TO FIGHT A DEATH MATCH ON LIVE TELEVISION, ONLY THE OTHER GUY WAS TOO MUCH OF A GUTLESS LITTLE PUNK TO SHOW UP!

Bob: "We went back to Hong Kong, and Chuck got challenged to a match. They didn't know I was coming, so I wasn't involved in it. And them, the way it was handled at, it wound up me accepting a death match on live TV with this idiot. And

they wanted to challenge Chuck Norris and Bruce said 'Heyyyy! You beat one guy and there's two. You beat two guys and there's four. You beat four and there's eight.' But Chuck was very upset. He's an intense competitor, and one of the toughest men on the planet. I mean, he is so tough. But he''s so kind, he doesn't ever have to tell you or show you. But I worked out with him so many times, I've got messed up shoulders from holding pads for this monster! So he wanted to go out and put this guy away, but Bruce said 'Please, don't take it any further. It's just going to get worse.' So Chuck had to suck it up. So we did what we always did: we got two rooms together and we cleaned out one room, shoved all the furniture out on the patio, and then that was our training center. And we did a viscous two hour workout, and the press was still there, so I finally realized he was getting upset – it was really eating him up that he couldn't go beat this guy's butt. So I called the guy Wang Bang – we'll let him remain nameless, as well, So I went to the press and said 'I'm Mr. Norris's student. Mr. Norris is way better than me. But I will accept the match with Wang Bang Lo on these conditions: That is be on live TV.' We're going on Enjoy Yourselves Tonight which almost everybody in Hong Kong watches and I'm gonna kill him! I'm gonna kill him dead. I want to kill him on live TV, because I don't want them to say that I poisoned him, or my two friends hit him in the leg with a bat or I got three other people to help me. I said 'The world's gonna see me kill Wang Bang Lo on live television! So, seven nights from tonight, Wang Bang, show up! And you're gonna die. So get your insurance, get your funeral, get everything arranged.' Well, we got there, there's thousands of people around the studio and where's Wang Bang Lo, the gutless little whit? Its like most people who bark, but they don't want to bite! So, he didn't show up, so the instructor – the director – was panicked, so he asked a couple of kung fu guys there to do a demonstration and a couple of Hapkido guys to do a demonstration and none of it was what he wanted. So he came and panicked to Chuck Norris, and he said, ' **I'VE GOT TO SEE SOME REAL FIGHTING! REAL FIGHTING!'** He was panicked. So the 'real fighting' got to be: Bob got to be the uke for Chuck! And I have pictures of that, where he's kicking the shit out of me! Just beating the hell out of me. Gave me one of my best

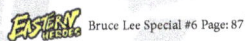

beatings! And its just... Chuck is amazing, and when he's pissed, he's like a Bruce Lee pissed! So the final thing he does is a jump spinning back kick BAM BAM!!! and I start falling into this black curtain! We didn't realize we were on stage, and I'm looking down at 20 feet of steel and spider webs, and I don't know to this day how Chuck did it – he's like, amazing! - because I'm falling, and he reached out and grabbed me - 190 pounds – I was 206, then, but he hit the stage so hard that it cut his hands right here, on his wrists. Just cut the hell out of em, real bad. But he pulled me up, and when he did, the gi came open, and the camera fades in and its got his footprints everywhere! [Bob slaps his chest and torso a few times.] I'm all red welts and they're like 'He doesn't have any padding!' I never wore padding. So that's how that happened."

THAT TIME WHEN BOB WALL HAD TO BEAT UP SAMMO HUNG ON THE SET OF GAME OF DEATH, KNOCK HIM OUT THREE TIMES AND KICK HIM OVER THE TOP ROPE, OUT OF THE RING, TO TEACH SAMMO A LESSON ABOUT WHAT A BADASS BOB WALL IS BECAUSE SAMMO HAD TO LEARN TO RESPECT HIM!

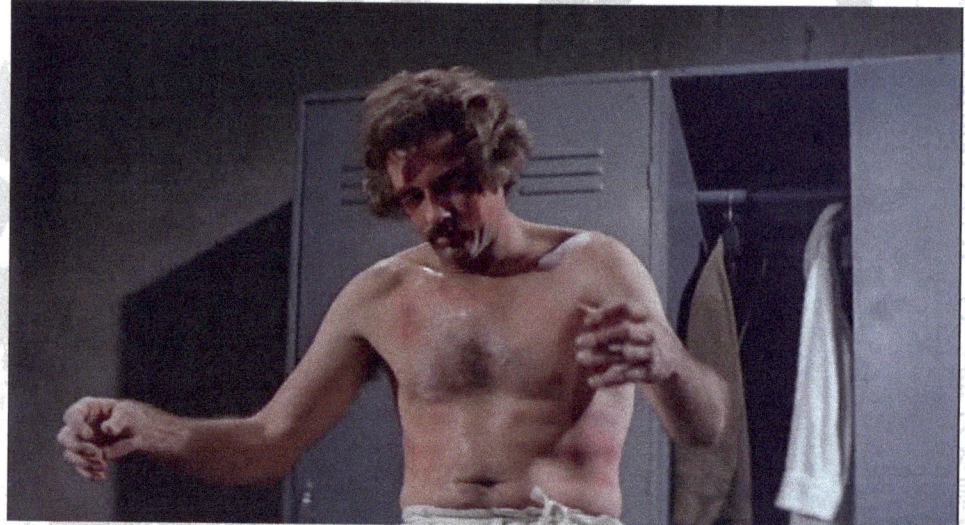

Bob: "Well, I love Sammo. Sammo and I got along very well when we did Enter the Dragon. But when we did Game of Death, four years later, he had become, I guess, pretty famous. I didn't know it. But when I got there, he wasn't reacting for me. So I knocked him out. And he didn't say anything. And in the next scene, I knocked him out again. Because, the Chinese kind of have an opinion like we're slow and stiff and stupid. If you're not Chinese, you're no good in a fight. I'll fight any of you, any time, any where, for any reason! Well, the third time I knocked him out, I side kicked him right over the ropes, right out of the ring and into the audience. He was out for five, six minutes. When he woke up that time, he had the interpreter ask me why I was knocking him out, and I got pictures of him – lumps everywhere, that I put on him. So, I wasn't liking him right then. But I got the interpreter over there, and I speak Cantonese, but I wanted to make sure he understood me, so I said to the interpreter, 'I had to take my lumps for Bruce Lee. After my name, it says Bob Wall, World Professional Karate Champion (Retired.) Look at my hands. Look at my face. I'm no punk. You wanna fight me? I'm here. Bring me your money, let it match your wallet!' So, I was kind of angry with him, because now, finally, my character gets to win! My character gets to do something. And he wasn't reacting. But, after the third time I knocked him out, his whole attitude changed. I said, 'I'm gonna keep knocking you out! If I have to knock you out eighty times, you're gonna get knocked out eighty times! You either better react well or I'll knock you out! You don't like it? Let's do it! We can film!' He decided to become my good buddy. So now I have pictures of him, arm in arm, best friends. And, actually, after that, he really is very talented. He gained a lot of weight between Enter the Dragon and Game of Death, but he's very athletic, he'd very – back flips. He can do all kinds of stuff. And he was marvelous after that. So, by the end of the filming, our friendship had come back again."

HOW BOB WALL HAD TO BEAT UP THE BRUCE LEE DOUBLE ON GAME OF DEATH TO TEACH HIM A LESSON ABOUT WHAT A BADASS BOB WALL IS, AND ALSO THAT GUY SUCKED AS A MARTIAL ARTIST AND ALSO DIRECTOR ROBERT CLOUSE IS AN ASSHOLE!

Bob: "Well, there were three guys. There was a Chinese guy who did the dialogue – he didn't look much like Bruce, but he could do the English dialogue. There was

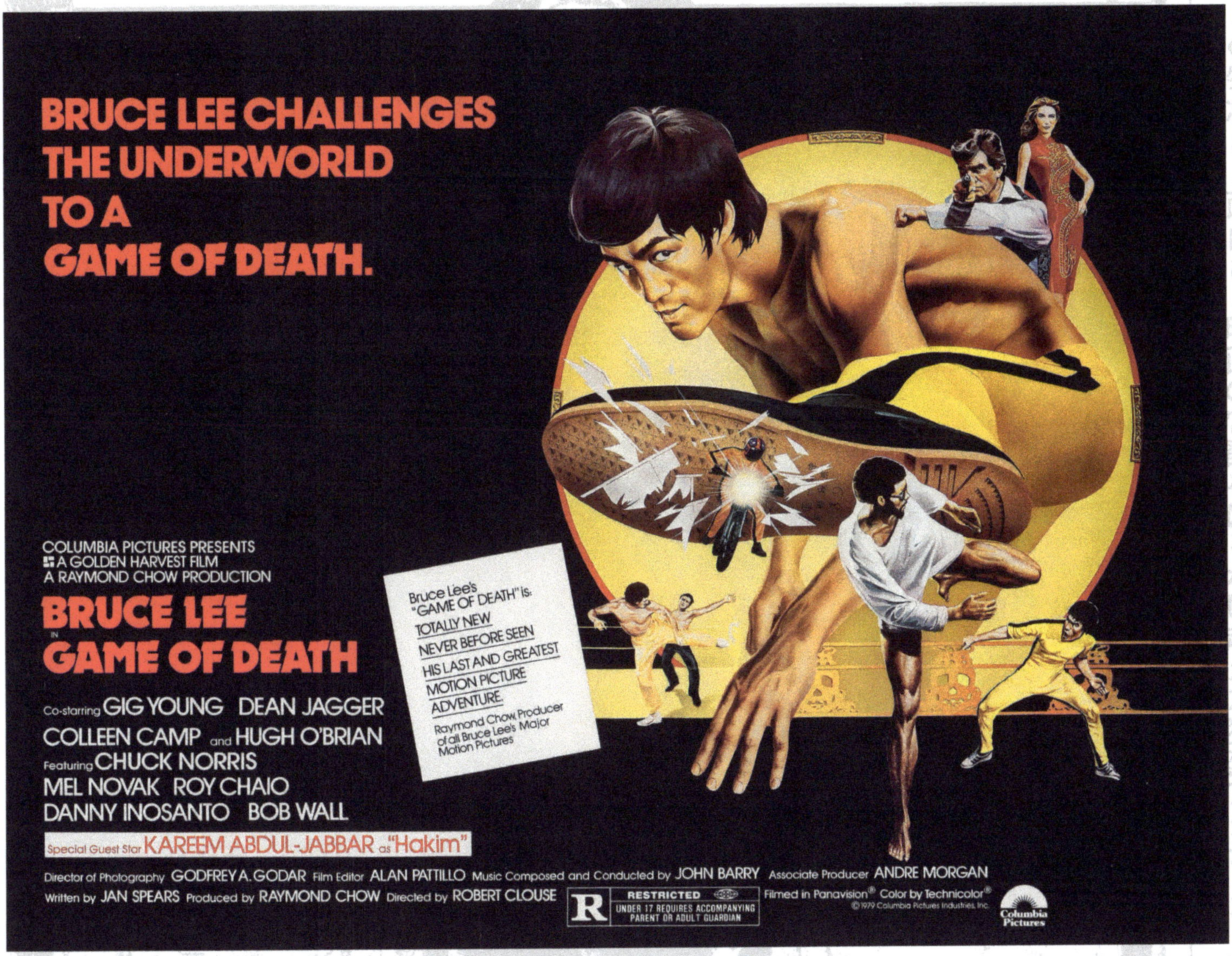
BRUCE LEE CHALLENGES THE UNDERWORLD TO A GAME OF DEATH.
COLUMBIA PICTURES PRESENTS
A GOLDEN HARVEST FILM
A RAYMOND CHOW PRODUCTION
BRUCE LEE IN GAME OF DEATH
Co-starring GIG YOUNG DEAN JAGGER
COLLEEN CAMP and HUGH O'BRIAN
Featuring CHUCK NORRIS
MEL NOVAK ROY CHAIO
DANNY INOSANTO BOB WALL
Special Guest Star KAREEM ABDUL-JABBAR as "Hakim"
Bruce Lee's "GAME OF DEATH" is: TOTALLY NEW NEVER BEFORE SEEN HIS LAST AND GREATEST MOTION PICTURE ADVENTURE.
Raymond Chow, Producer of all Bruce Lee's Major Motion Pictures
Director of Photography GODFREY A. GODAR Film Editor ALAN PATTILLO Music Composed and Conducted by JOHN BARRY Associate Producer ANDRE MORGAN
Written by JAN SPEARS Produced by RAYMOND CHOW Directed by ROBERT CLOUSE
R RESTRICTED UNDER 17 REQUIRES ACCOMPANYING PARENT OR ADULT GUARDIAN
Filmed in Panavision® Color by Technicolor®
©1979 Columbia Pictures Industries, Inc.
Columbia Pictures

another fellow that was Chinese who just did motorcycle stuff. He did dangerous stunts. There was another fellow – a Korean – that I taught, that was also a wise-ass when I got him, until I took him to the gym and educated his ass. And he thought he was some deadly Taekwondo 4th degree or something – I don't know what he thought he was – but once he understood 'I can beat you up any time I want! I can beat you up and your instructor and your instructor's instructor and all of their friends at the same time!' So, we had to get past that same ego crap. But, once I did that... he wasn't a very good martial artist. It was very difficult, because he would never hit you in the same spot. He's supposed to hit you there, he hits you here, he hits you there he hits you there. You know, Bruce hit you exactly where he was supposed to. So that was very different. But, like I said, after I educated him, he became nice to me. He was first disrespectful, until I educated him. But he was, in my opinion, not the best choice. I think he was an incompetent martial artist. Another reason it was very difficult to make that film as good as it was. I mean, I had to do a lot of my own – I had to throw my own kicks and shoot em over my hip, because he couldn't do it. I had to beat myself up! I had to throw myself into the locker. So, I don't think he was the wisest choice. Nice guy but – c'mon! It's comparatively tough to be onscreen with Gene Lebell, with Bruce Lee – You've got the greatest martial artist in the history of cinematic Earth, as far as I'm concerned. So I understood the challenge. But again, Clouse picked him. It goes right back to Bob Clouse: asshole, idiot and lousy director!"

WHY GAME OF DEATH SHOULD HAVE BEEN BETTER!

Bob: "It could have been really good! Really, really good! But Clouse was just... You know, my most enjoyable memory... First of all, I loved everybody on the film. And I love Fred Weintraub – been a partner and a good friend – and I got to take my wife, that was the first time, it was the only film she got to go with me on. And my oldest daughter. And, so I got paid a lot of money, so it made it really pleasurable. And, they called me back, after my prediction came true. I left there in something like September of '77. I finished. And Andre Morgan called me, and he said, 'Bob, you were right. Clouse has ruined the fight scenes. We need you to come back and re-shoot the whole locker sequence!' Which I created. And I said, 'OK, but I want double what I was getting before!' And it was an awesome, scary amount before! 'And each week they keep me there, it doubles. And I want first class airfare for my wife, my eldest daughter and me and a suite, a language instructor!' And they said 'Yes.' And I said 'Oh, one other condition: Bob Clouse cannot be in the country. Because if he's in the country, I'm gonna put him in the hospital! Because I do not like him, and

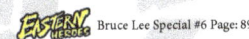

I'm not gonna let that weasel ruin it again! I told you in advance on the phone and by mail, he will ruin the fight scenes. He's an idiot. And the only reason he got this credit for being the director of Enter the Dragon was Bruce Lee's genius, not his genius!' Bruce Lee put those fight scenes on film. He directed them. So I said that's the condition: 'No Bob Clouse! But, one other condition: I want Sammo Hung.' Sammo came and did a phenomenal job! I mean, Sammo really is talented. He's very talented. And he and I created the fight scenes. Which I think, the locker room fight scenes, considering we didn't have Bruce there, we just had a little bit of clips to use. And we could only access what Clouse had allowed us to access. But, considering that, I believe the Game of Death fight scene is one of the best ever put on film. I think its up there with Chuck Norris's film with Bruce and Bruce's and mine in Enter the Dragon. If you go look at it, there's a lot of good stuff in there, and let me tell ya, holding somebody like this and having him kick backwards? That's not easy. So, I was pleased with it, thanks to Sammo. Because Sammo – by then, we had a great mutual respect, and Sammo, he knows his stuff!"

WHY ACCIDENTALLY CUTTING BRUCE LEE WITH BROKEN BOTTLES IN ENTER THE DRAGON TOTALLY WASN'T BOB WALL'S FAULT, BUT WAS, INSTEAD, JUST AN ACCIDENT AND ALSO ROBERT CLOUSE'S FAULT AND ALSO ROBERT CLOUSE IS AN ASSHOLE AND THAT'S WHY BOB HAD TO BEAT HIM UP AND THREATEN HIM!

Bob: "Well, what happened is very simple. Anybody who knows anything about martial arts – well, first of all, Bruce is kicking me with a kick I taught him – a crescent kick. OK? Standing right leg forward. His instructions to me were, 'Bob, I want you to break the bottles, take the one in your right hand, and I want you to try to stab me in the pec. If you can stab me in the pec, do it! Come as fast as you can! Try to stab me in the pec! My right pec! Right hand, right pec!' That's my instructions. Bruce was a no kidding around martial artist and knew the risk – he knew we were using real bottles. So, nobody stopped to think that, when I break those bottles, I gotta fall on

that glass, and I can't look around and say, 'Oh, there's a big piece, I think I'll fall over here!' That's why my uniform got shredded. The last one, I still have – shredded in the back. We do it perfectly! Now, the way the scene – if you know anything about martial arts, he's gonna do a crescent kick, and he's coming with his right leg inside out, and he catches me between the wrist and the elbow, bottle flies away. Take a look at the scene again and see how hard he hits my arm! You can see it and hear it! Its no kidding around! He was full force cracking me! Six times, perfect! Seventh time, I'm getting faster each time, missed timing, he catches me behind the elbow, the bottle doesn't move, he jams his own fist into it. Missed timing. It was the risk we both took. Made me feel really bad. I'm there because I love Bruce. I'm there for a serious cut in pay. Last thing I want is for Bruce to get hurt, to be embarrassed in front of the whole set, blood spurting out of his hand. Stitches! Off for a week! So, I felt bad then, I feel bad now. But, Bruce and I understood – we were professionals! We knew that Clouse had us use real glass instead of fake glass that we should have been using, but he wanted us to get hurt, if that was possible, because he's a jerk! And I'll say that again: Bob Clouse did not like Bruce Lee or Bob Wall! If you want to know, I can show you my original script with all the names like 'Braithwaite,' which Bruce couldn't say, but Bruce took em all out, but he left that one in, just as his way of saying, 'OK, I'm gonna let you have one on me.' But Clouse was not a nice man. He's an insecure, inadequate, petty director, who got his reputation from Bruce Lee doing it for him! So, anyway, I'm sitting in my hotel room – we can't shoot for a week. Fred Weintraub came and said, 'Hey, you gotta leave Hong Kong!' I said 'Why do I have to leave Hong Kong?' 'Well, there's a rumor Bruce is gonna kill you when we start shooting again!' I said, 'Well, first of all, Bruce and I have been close friends for almost 11 years, and training partners. Second of all, after my name, it says Bob Wall, World Professional Champion (Retired.) It doesn't say that after Bruce's name. Next, Bruce on a wet day weighs 150 pounds, five seven. I'm six feet tall, 206 pounds!' I was around 190, but I went up for that film. 'And, more importantly than all that, we love each other! We're really close friends!' I said, 'Its total BS! Let's go to Bruce's house right now!' Freddie and I went to Bruce's house. Freddie tells him the rumor. Bruce gets on the phone. He calls five or six people, in Cantonese: 'Where did this rumor come from?' 'Bob Clouse!' 'Where did the rumor come from?' 'Bob Clouse!' He said, 'They're all coming from Bob Clouse!' Well, Bruce hated that BS! He didn't like BS at all. He was a very direct guy. If he didn't like you, he would tell you. And he didn't like BS, and I think he was insulted as much as I was that he was spreading this rumor. So, Bruce said 'Let's go see him!' So, Bruce and I jumped in the car – Bruce's red Mercedes – back to my hotel, where Clouse was in another suite. We opened the door, and as soon as Clouse opened the door, I slapped him, right on top of his head! And it was not a kindly slap – he fell on the ground! I stood on his hand. I said, 'You are spreading a rumor that Bruce is gonna kill me! Bruce,

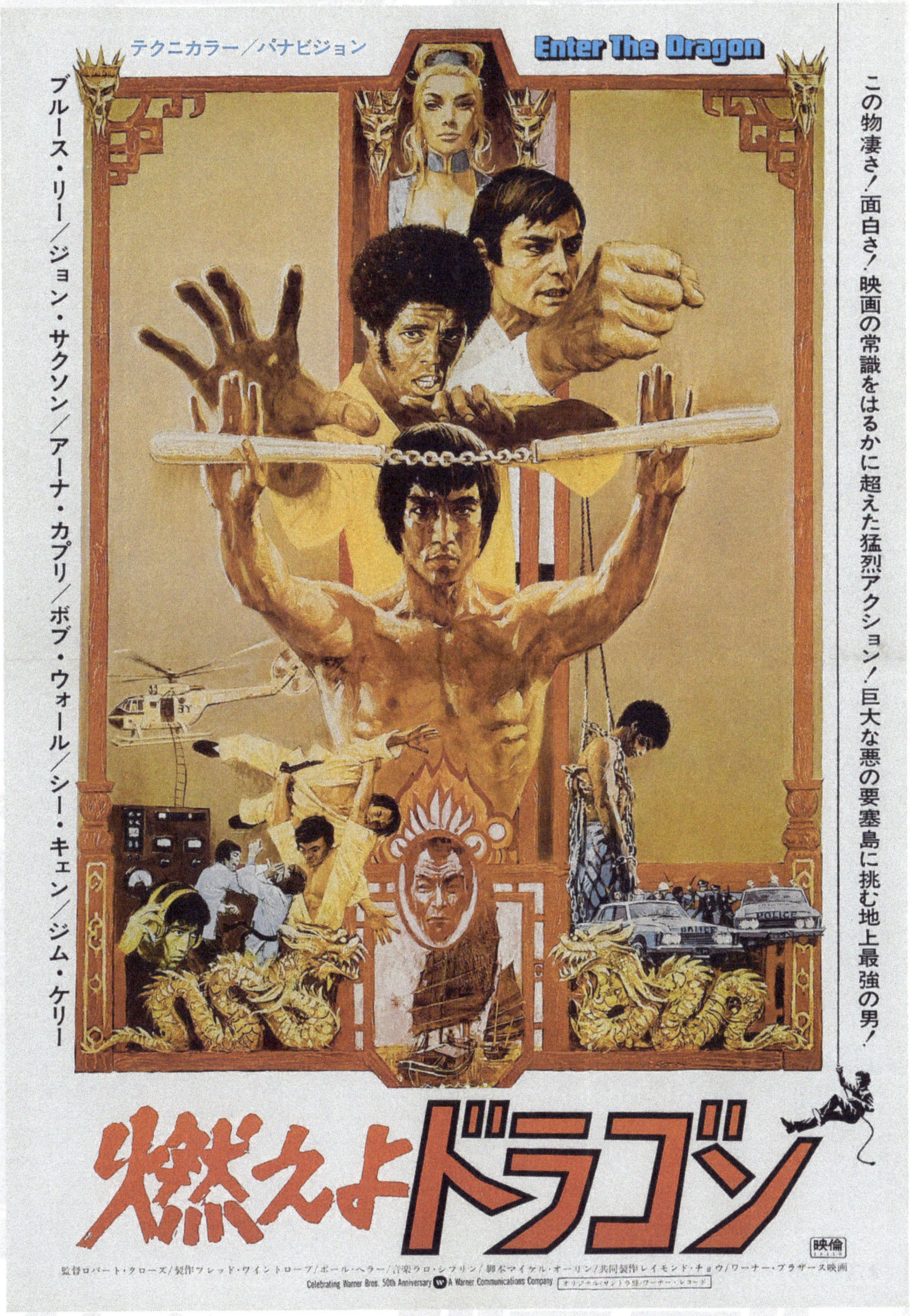

テクニカラー／パナビジョン
Enter The Dragon
この物凄さ！面白さ！映画の常識をはるかに超えた猛烈アクション！巨大な悪の要塞島に挑む地上最強の男！
ブルース・リー／ジョン・サクソン／アーナ・カプリ／ボブ・ウォール／シー・キェン／ジム・ケリー
燃えよドラゴン
映倫
監督ロバート・クローズ／製作フレッド・ワイントローブ／ポール・ヘラー／音楽ラロ・シフリン／脚本マイケル・オーリン／共同製作レイモンド・チョウ／ワーナー・ブラザース映画
Celebrating Warner Bros. 50th Anniversary A Warner Communications Company

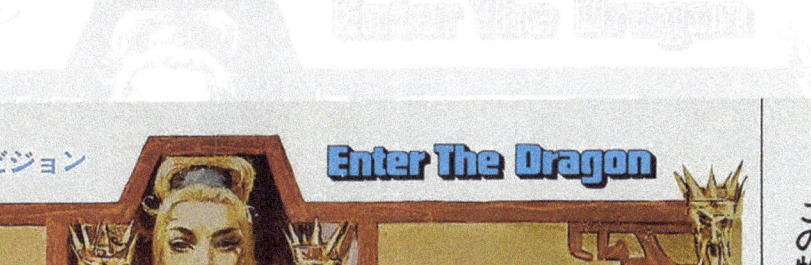

are you gonna kill me?' **'NO WAY, YOU SOB, AND IT STOPS NOW!'** I said, 'If the rumor continues, I'm gonna put you in the hospital! And you will NOT be directing anything, not even traffic! Goodbye!' Rumor over! So, it was a complete falsehood. It was BS! And, at the end of the day, what's the proof? We went back to the 7th shot, and Bruce hit me exactly where he was supposed to! Hit me so hard that the guy got his arm broken behind me because he was jerking around! He was stupid enough to believe that Bruce was gonna kill me. Could he have killed me? I'm not blocking – what if Bruce had kicked me in the throat or the face? I probably wouldn't be here to talk to you right now. But Bruce did what he always did – hit me exactly where he was supposed to! Yes, just slightly harder, if that's possible, but... nah. It was all BS."

BOB WALL RECALLS WHAT A SHITTY DRIVER BRUCE LEE WAS!

Bob: "We were out filming Black Belt Jones when Linda called Fred Weintraub and I went with him to the phone, just to say hello, and found out he had died. And the very first thought that hit my head was: Bruce was the WORST driver on the planet! He was the best martial artist, the worst driver! You're driving with Bruce... [Bob mimes bad steering and driving] So, anyways, 'Oh my god! A car accident!' Cause I can't even tell you how many cars he crashed!"

HOW BOB WALL DECIDED NOT TO BECOME A HUGE MOVIE STAR IN ORDER TO MAKE HIS WIFE HAPPY AND ALSO HE KNOWS A LOT OF FAMOUS PEOPLE AND WOMEN STILL THROW THEMSELVES AT HIM!

Bob: "Well, you know, Warner Brothers offered me a three picture, starring role, same as they did Jim Kelly. They were so impressed with our roles in Enter the Dragon. And, at that point, I was pretty excited about starring roles, and it was pretty good money – each one went way up! But my wife said 'If you sign that contract, we're gonna get a divorce! You have to decide if you want to be a married man or a movie star. You're going to make as much money doing what you do in real estate – you're very good at it – but, you've always said: Every heterosexual man I've ever met is a whore at heart! God gave us eyes, we see T&A, we love it! But, some men grow up and mature and give up childish toys. I'm one of those guys. I've been married 44 years. I'm in love with my wife. I'm crazy in love with my wife. And I've never fallen off the wagon – I'm a recovering whore for 44 years! My eyes have still – God still left them with me, so I still see things I'd love to have, but I'm not gonna go for childish toys when I've got the best woman on the planet: my wife at home, the mother of my two beautiful daughters. So, I have never regretted – although we went about a month before I finally told Warner Brothers I wasn't going to do the deal. I was mad at her. I thought she robbed me off the opportunity to be a star. And she kept reminding me: 'Look, every star you've ever taught, from Elvis, Jack Palance, Brian Keith, Paul Newman, Freddie Prinze, Steve McQueen - every one of 'em wound up with divorces or problems in their marriages! Because, do you believe that I believe that you're going to be on a movie set for three months, I'm gonna be home with the children and you're not gonna have sex? You're an admitted whore, and you've got all those groupies there that wanna do ya, whether you're handsome or studly or anything else, you're the star, you're making a lot of money, and they want to be in that

life! So, there's going to be girls throwing themselves at you!' Look, I'm 73 and they're still throwing themselves at me! So, the answer is, I didn't further my film career because of my wife, and she made the right decision for us, because I'm still married! I'm still in love."

About the Author:

Jason McNeil is an actor, writer and martial artist who has appeared in numerous movies and television shows, including as host of Stars-Stunts-Action! - taking you behind the scenes of action movies and martial arts entertainment! - now streaming on Tubi! He also once got to meet the late, great Bob Wall, but did not, as so many of his martial arts heroes did before him, get to kick Bob in the balls.

BOB WALL PHOTO GALLERY

テクニカラー／パナビジョン

Enter The Dragon

ブルース・リー　ジョン・サクソン　アーナ・カプリ　ボブ・ウォール　シー・キエン　ジム・ケリー

この物凄さ！面白さ！映画の常識をはるかに超えた猛烈アクション！巨大な要塞島に挑む地上最強の男！

燃えよドラゴン

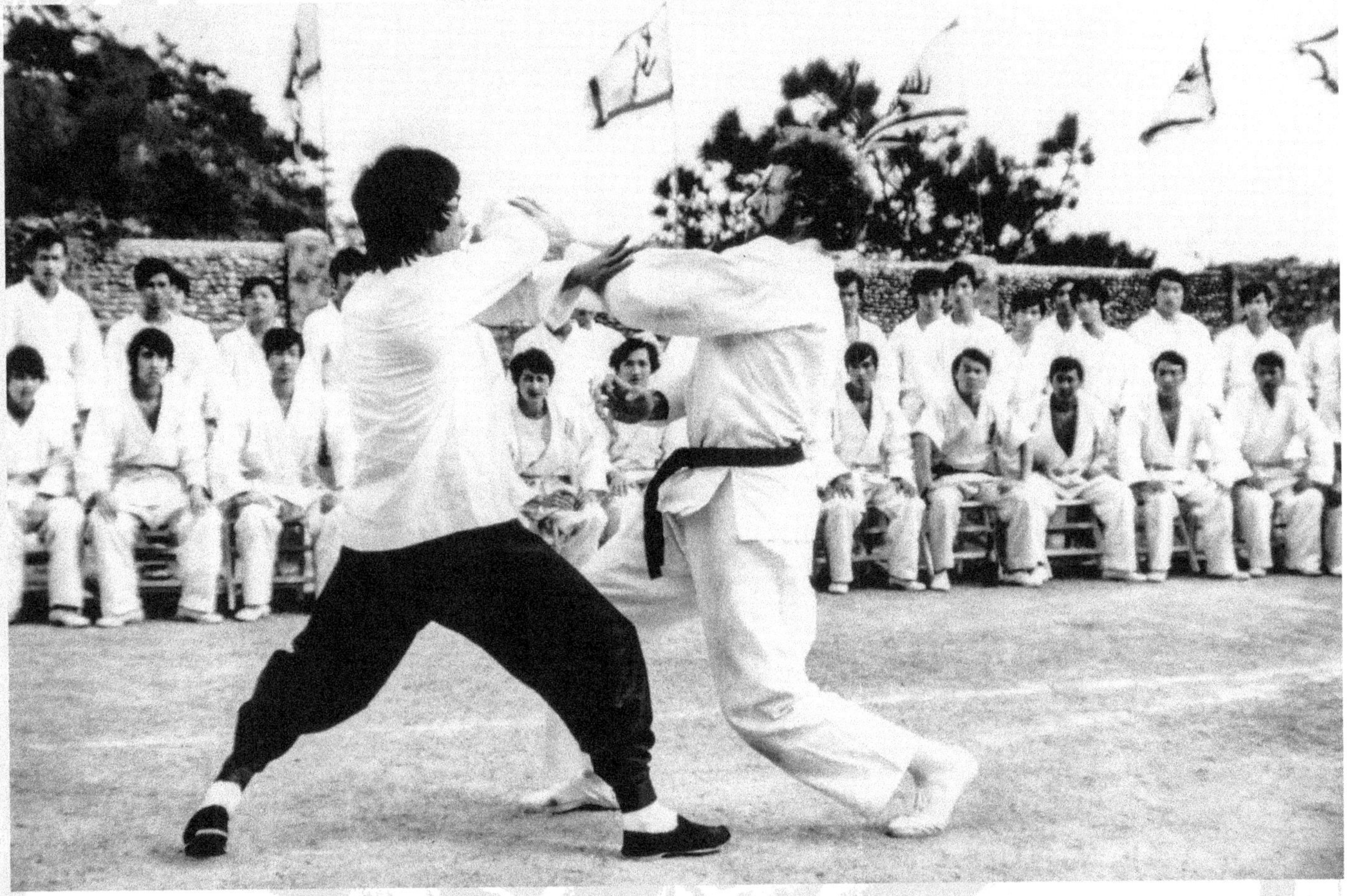

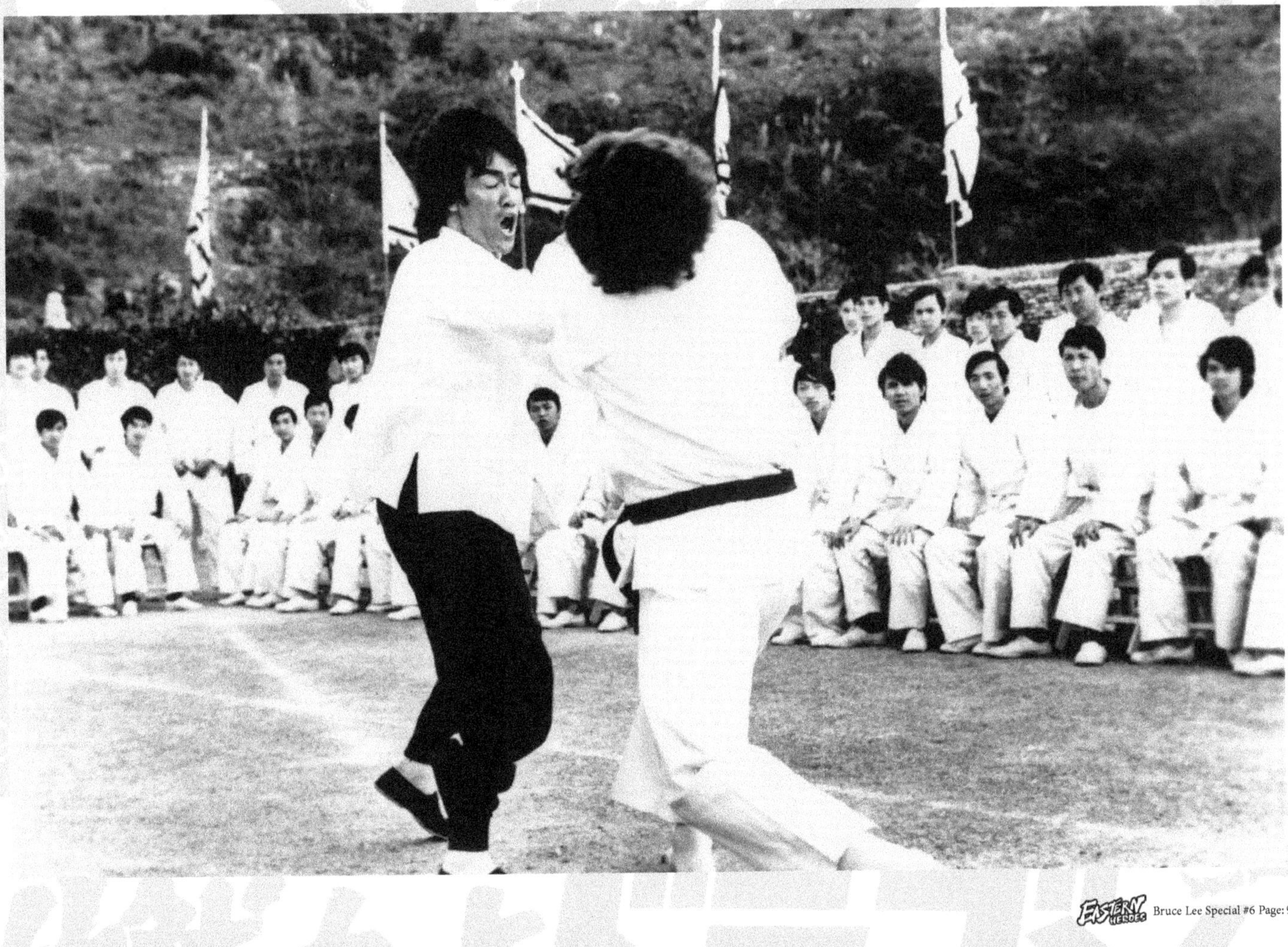

テクニカラー パナビジョン　　　　　　Enter The Dragon

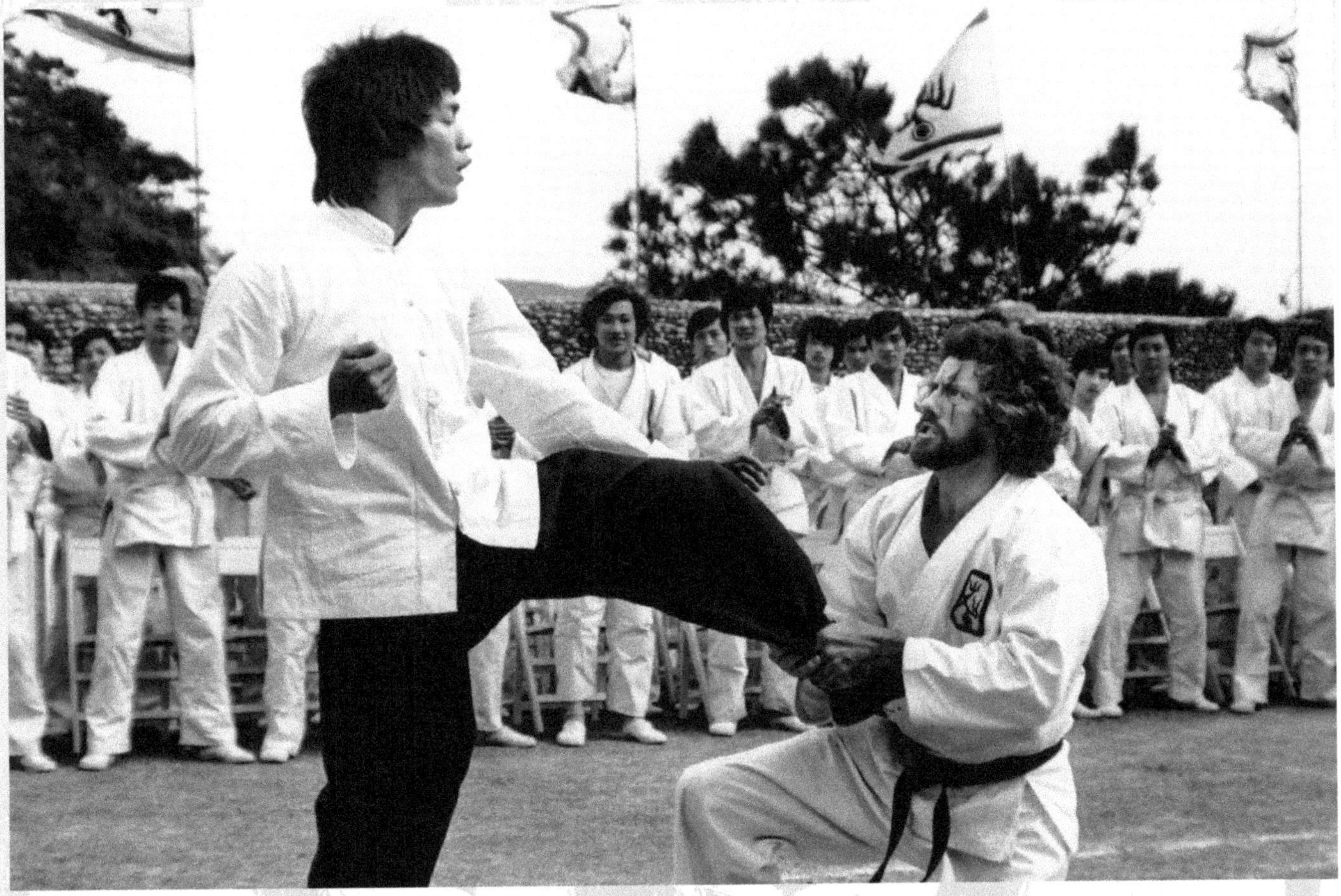

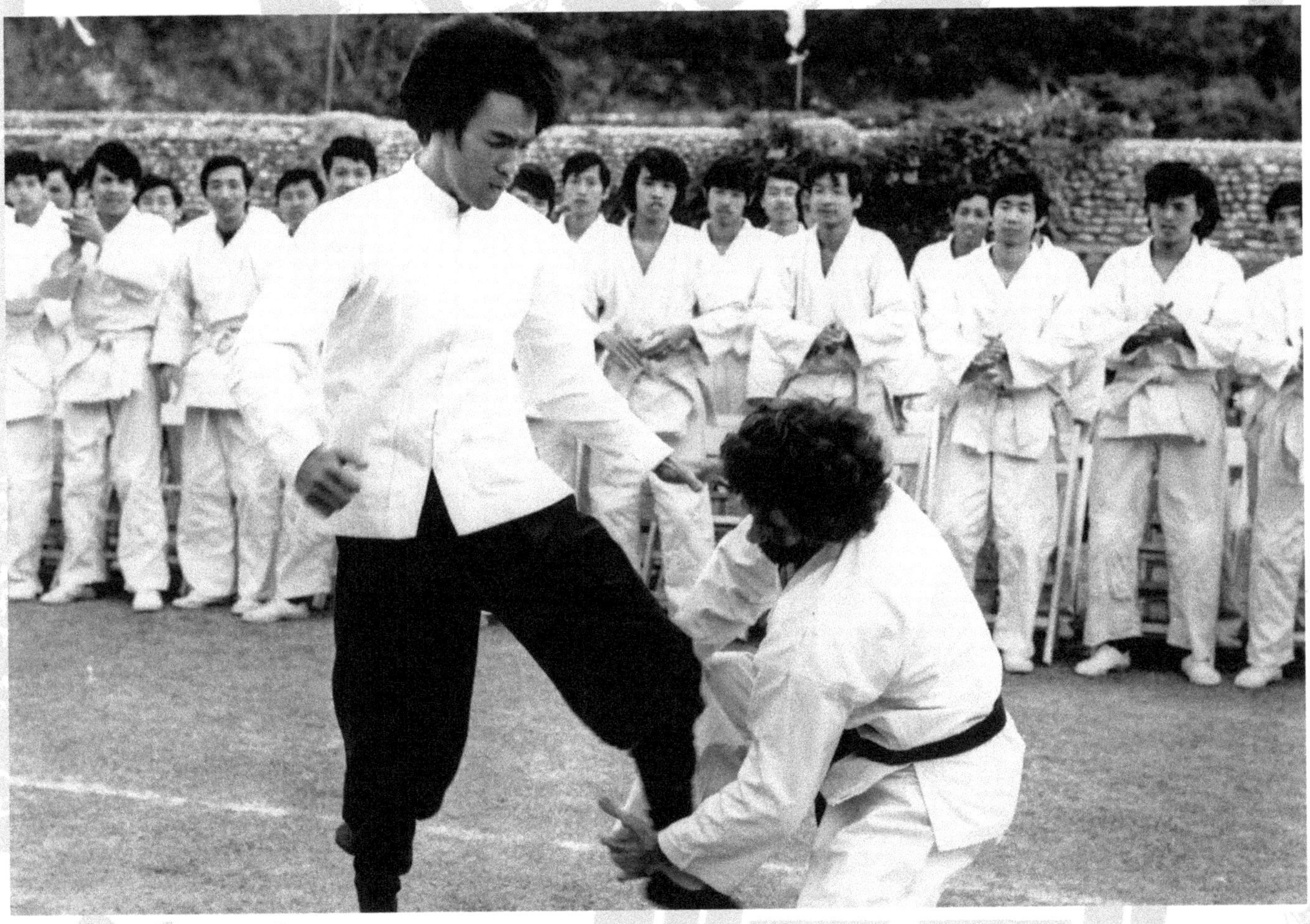

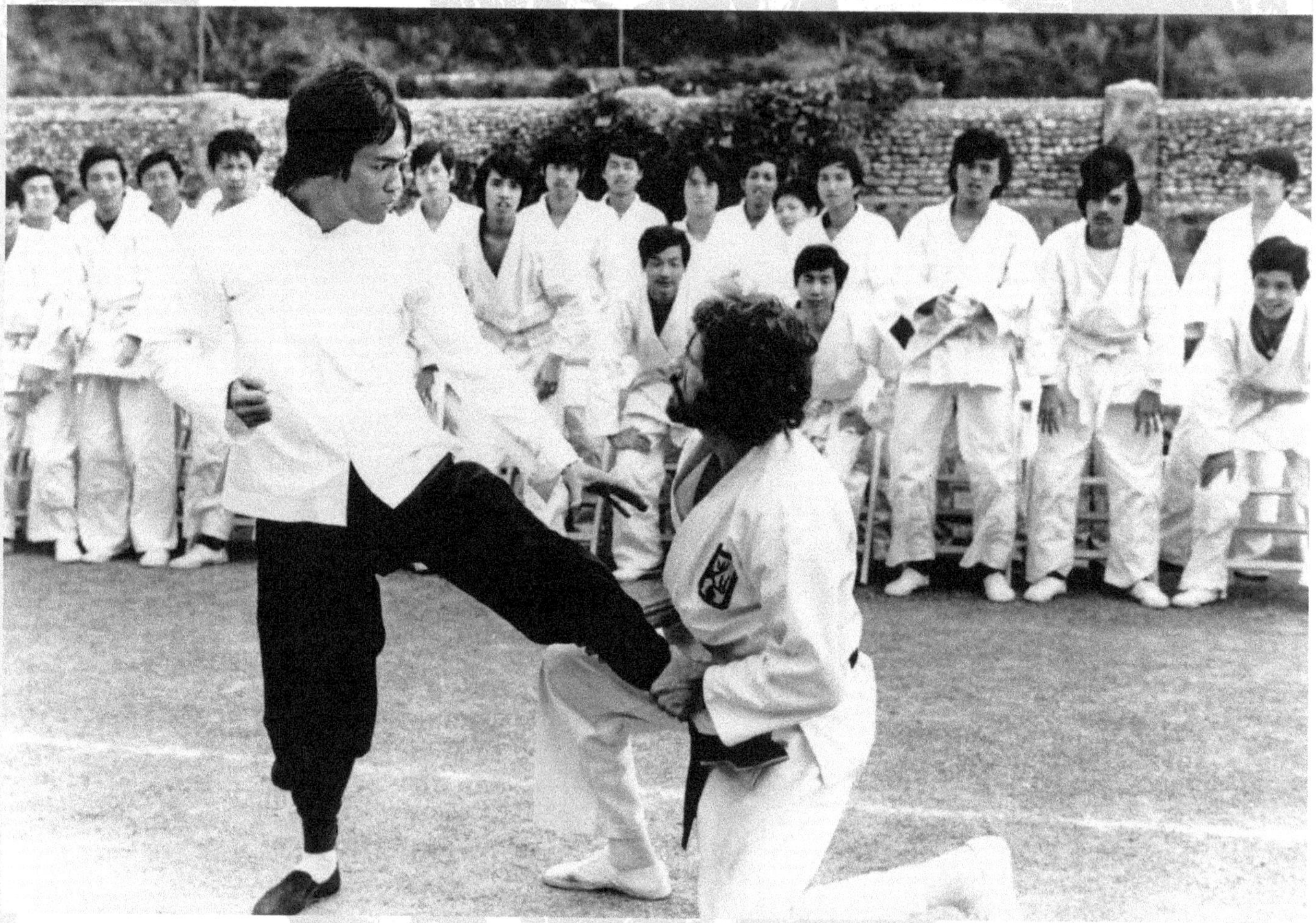

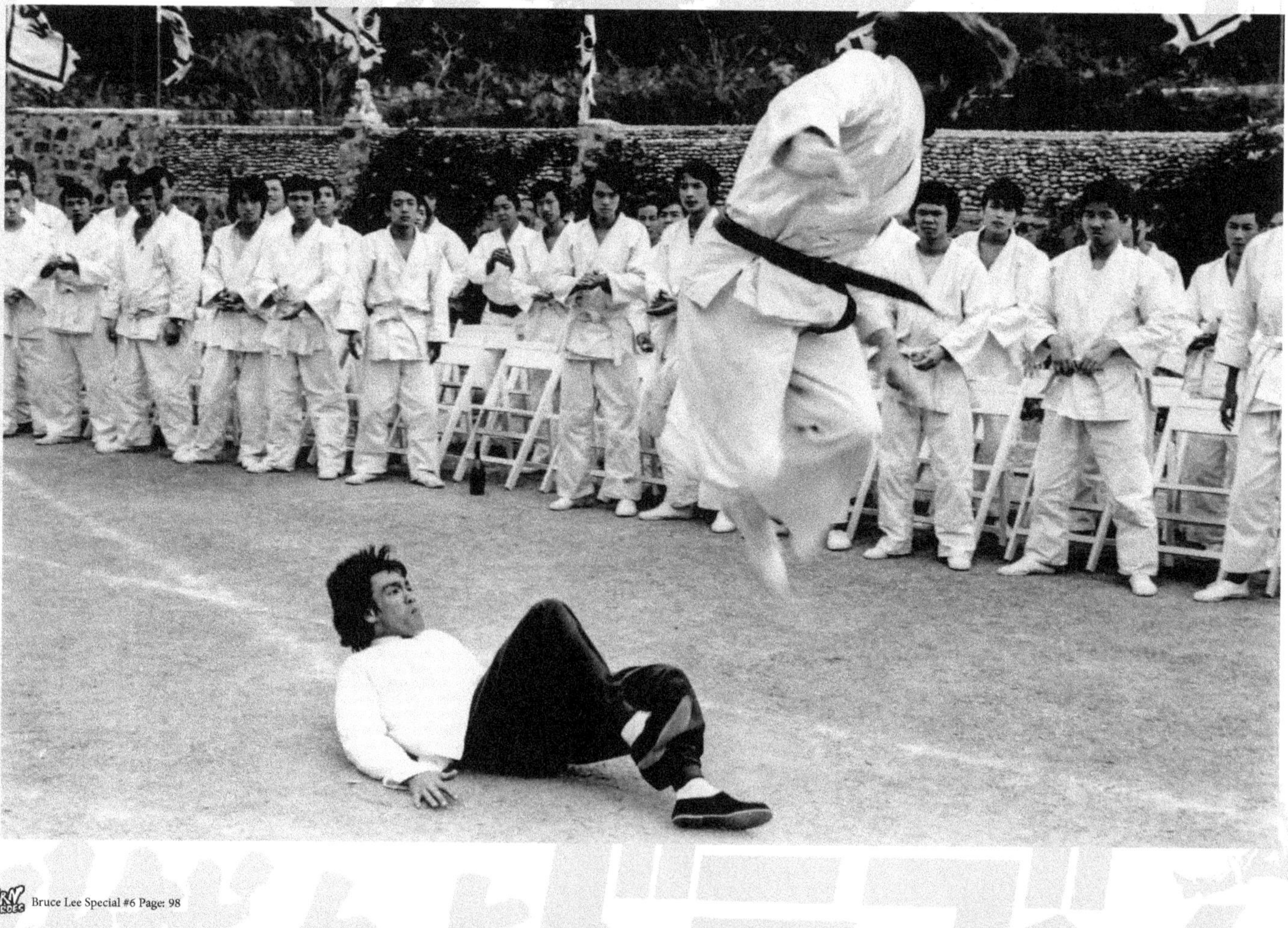

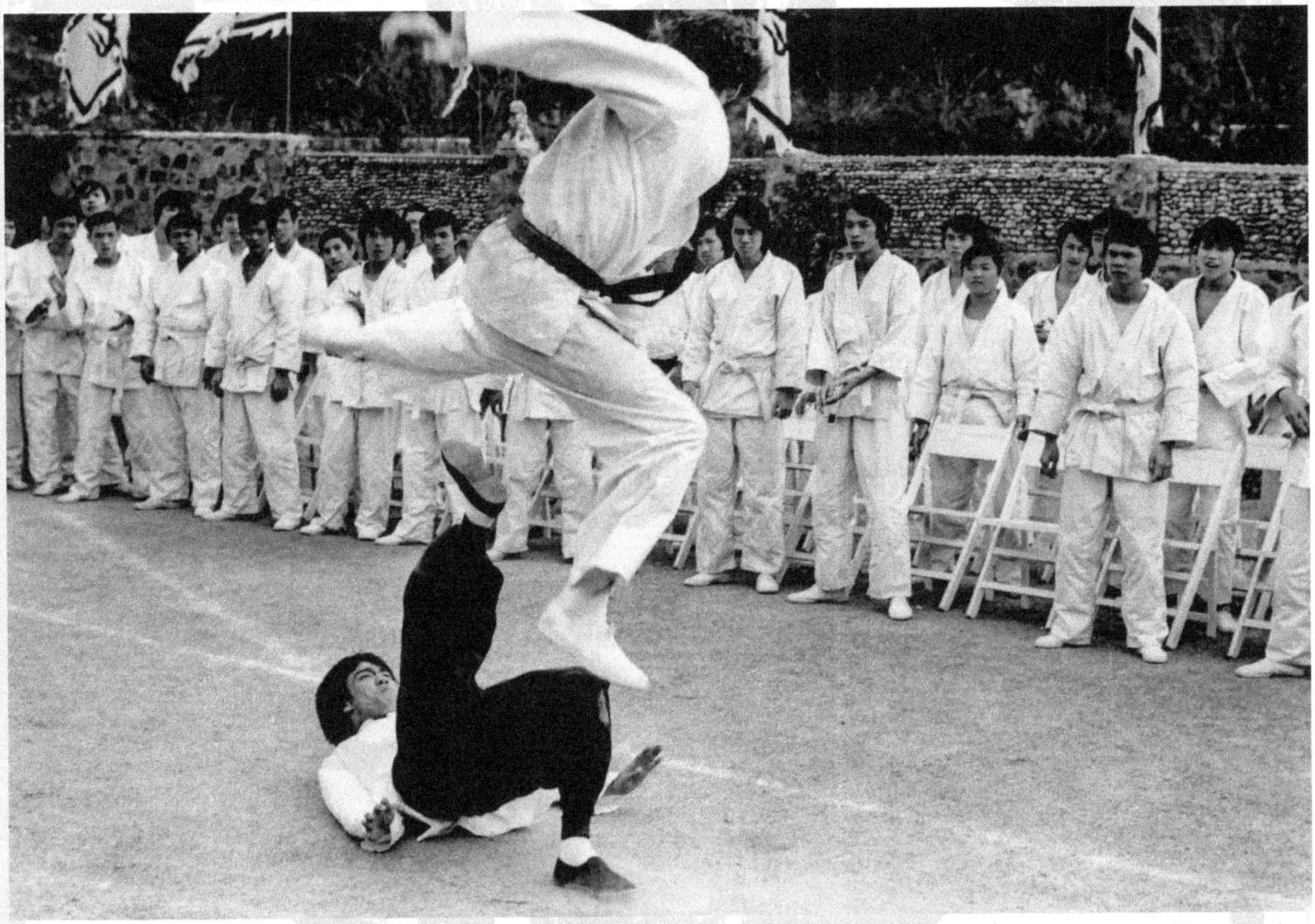

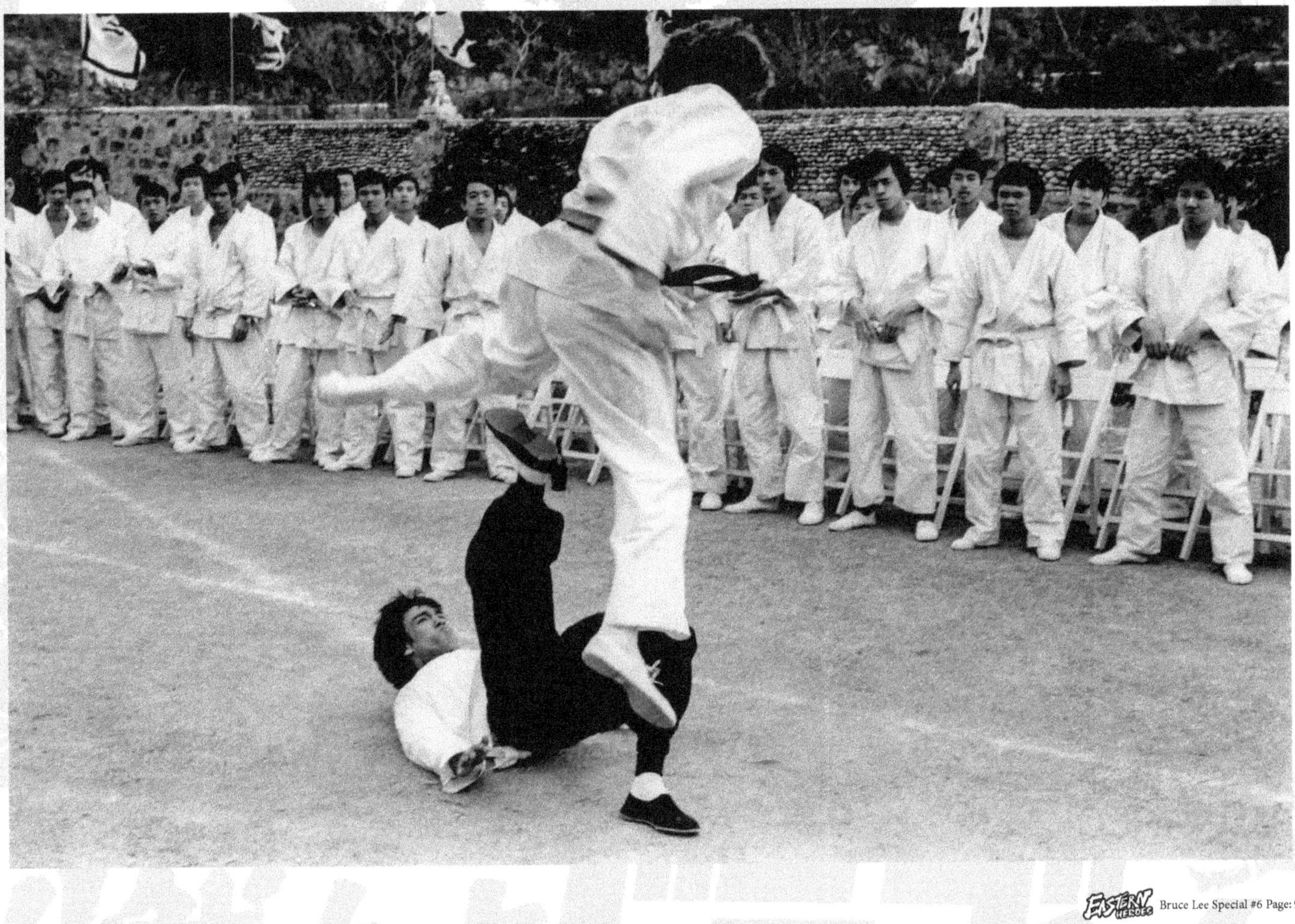

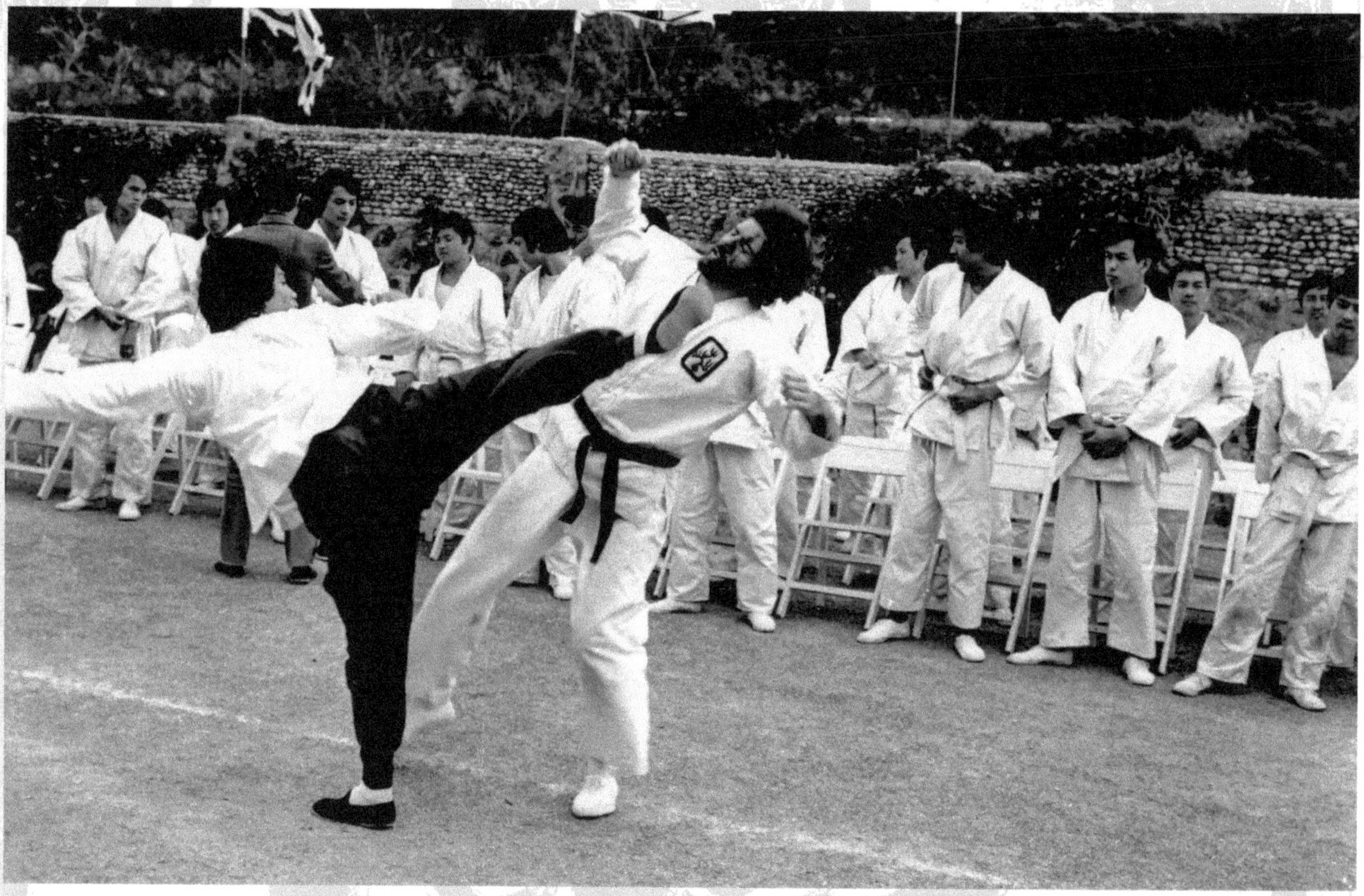

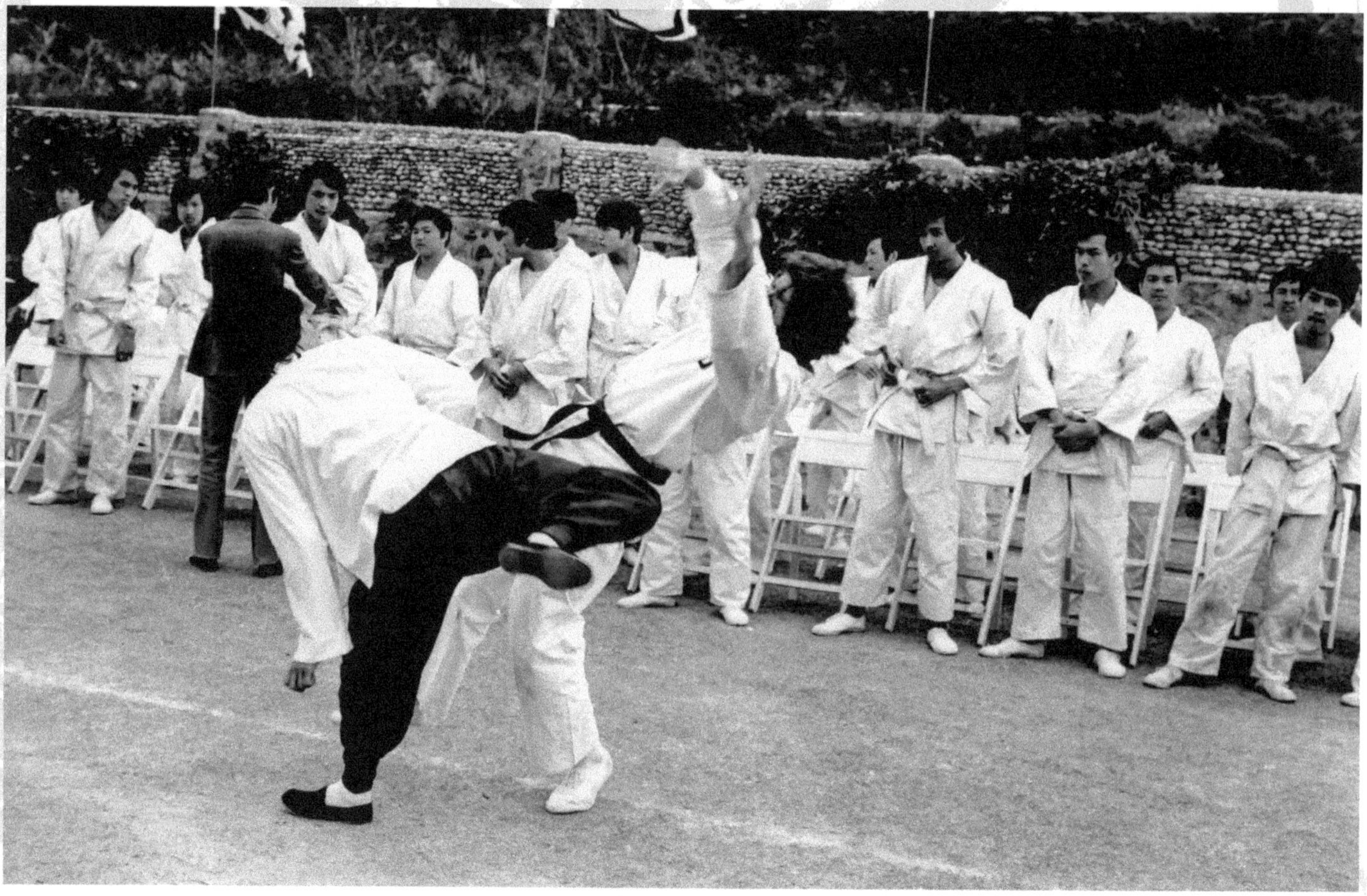

THANK YOU'S

COMPILED & EDITED BY RICK BAKER
DESIGNED BY TIM HOLLINGSWORTH

CONTRIBUTORS

MIKE NESBITT (UK)
CHRIS EVANS (UK)
SIMON PRITCHARD (UK)
ALAN DONKIN (UK)
JOHNNY BURNETT (UK)
JEFF BONA (USA)
MIKE KELLY (USA)
JOHN NEGRON (USA)
JASON MCNEIL (USA)
PETER GEISSLER (AUSTRIA)

Eastern Heroes© is a registered trade mark

www.ingramcontent.com/pod-product-compliance
Lightning Source LLC
Chambersburg PA
CBHW061125170426
43209CB00013B/1671